Library Centers

LIBRARY CENTERS

Teaching Information Literacy, Skills, and Processes: K-6

JUDITH A. SYKES

Drawings by Cory Henderson

1997
LIBRARIES UNLIMITED, INC.
and Its Division
Teacher Ideas Press
Englewood, Colorado

Copyright © 1997 Judith A. Sykes
All Rights Reserved
Printed in the United States of America

No part of this publication may be reproduced, stored in a retrieval system, or transmitted, in any form or by any means, electronic, mechanical, photocopying, recording, or otherwise, without the prior written permission of the publisher. An exception is made for individual librarians and educators, who may make copies of activity sheets for classroom use in a single school. Other portions of the book (up to 15 pages) for use in a single school or library. Standard citation information should appear on each page.

Libraries Unlimited, Inc.
and Its Division
Teacher Ideas Press
P.O. Box 6633
Englewood, CO 80155-6633
1-800-237-6124
www.lu.com

Production Editor: Kay Mariea
Copy Editor: Brooke Graves
Proofreader: Susie Sigman
Typesetter: Kay Minnis

Library of Congress Cataloging-in-Publication Data

Sykes, Judith A., 1957-
    Library centers : teaching information literacy, skills, and processes,
K-6 / Judith A. Sykes ; drawings by Cory Henderson.
    xiv, 224 p. 22x28 cm.
    ISBN 1-56308-507-0
    1. Library orientation for school children--United States. 2. Library
orientation for school children--Canada. I. Title.
Z711.2.S98   1997
025.5'678222--dc21   97-7093
                                                            CIP

This book is dedicated to my daughter, Michelle;
our children are our future.

Center time!

Contents

Preface ix
Acknowledgments xi
Introduction xiii

Chapter 1—
ABC BEARS 1

Chapter 2—
ABC BOOKWORMS 15

Chapter 3—
BRIDGE BOOKS 29

Chapter 4—
JUNIOR AUTHORS 41

Chapter 5—
RATTLING READERS 53

Chapter 6—
BOOK BASICS 63

Chapter 7—
VICTORIAN HOLIDAY TRADITIONS 77

Chapter 8—
EGYPT OLD AND NEW 89

Chapter 9—
ANCIENT GREECE 103

vii

Chapter 10—
TITANIC 115

Chapter 11—
SPACE 129

Chapter 12—
NATIVES 139

Chapter 13—
NATURAL RESOURCES 149

Chapter 14—
HISTORY 100 163

Chapter 15—
LINKS WITHIN BORDERS 177

Chapter 16—
REGIONS 189

Chapter 17—
EXPLORATION 201

Chapter 18—
LINKS ACROSS BORDERS 213

Chapter 19—
CENTER TIPS 223

viii

Preface

Resource-based library centers have proven to be an effective teaching strategy in schools to enhance student learning. Cooperatively planned with classroom teachers and continually revised to meet current student needs and changing technologies, the centers approach allows for hands-on activities in the school library by small groups with a high learner/adult ratio. Constructivist learning theory shows that learners build knowledge structures rather than receive them. The centers approach to resource-based learning provides the teacher-librarian and teacher with many opportunities to model appropriate learning behaviors, guide student activities, and provide various examples as student knowledge builds. One of the major factors of educational reform is collaboration; planning, implementing, and evaluating instructional activities jointly leads to change and professional growth. These skills are developed as a teacher or teaching team work together on activities with the teacher-librarian.

Although centers are not the sole instructional method in the library program, they can become an underlying structure for program continuity. This book documents a continuous program that can be used in an elementary school. Colleagues teaching at the secondary level might benefit from library centers for planning structures and may be able to use or adapt some of the more challenging research topics presented in this book (such as Victorian Holiday Traditions in chapter 7, the Titanic unit in chapter 10, or the social studies topics in chapters 13 through 18).

Teachers need to ensure a smooth flow from classroom preparation activities through follow-up, including homework and evaluation procedures. In this book, teachers are challenged to attempt diverse methodologies and to build on current educational philosophies. These philosophies, suggested by respected educators such as Nancy Atwell and Donald Graves, advocate repeated series of "mini-lessons"; they also stress the need for learners of all ages to have a great amount and variety of experiences with fiction and non-fiction, rather than the traditional lengthy "report." Fine arts activities and activities incorporating technology in learning are included in this multisensory approach.

Students have responded enthusiastically to this approach in the library and demonstrate much success in learning skills and strategies in their growth toward becoming information-independent. They look forward to new library centers and rotating to different activities within library centers. They eagerly provide direct or indirect feedback into planning library centers. They also benefit from another important aspect of learning: socialization and group culture, which give the benefits of discussion, discourse, and shared creativity.

ix

Acknowledgments

This book reflects the collaborative efforts of many colleagues over the years 1985 to 1996 in the Calgary Public Board of Education. Most notable is the staff of Southwood Elementary School, under the leadership of Principal Nestor Yaremko, who also did the photography for this book. I hope that *Library Centers* will serve as a vehicle for active, authentic resource-based learning.

Poring over books

Introduction

Library Centers developed from a cooperatively planned learning continuum based on strategies that allow the student to prepare to interact with a wide variety of resources, to create and share the results of that interaction to show they understand the process, and to reflect upon those results. Each teacher in the school contributed to these centers with strategies being implemented in a variety of ways. A consistently successful strategy emerged—namely, centers—which provide a continuous program in which each class in the school participates. Library centers are connected to the classroom with a literature or research theme or other curricular link. Learners could participate in a minimum of two such units in the school library per year. Some learners participate in additional library centers, independent studies, or book or author projects; they receive more library-related time during which skills developed in centers can flourish and foster further independence.

In most cases, a group of teachers and the teacher-librarian plan the activities so that learners can complete tasks with a degree of independence or minimal individualized instruction. At least two adults—the teacher and the teacher-librarian—plan and deliver the program, through which learners are assisted as needed, encouraged, remediated, or enriched. In many cases, when having an adult present at all times would enhance learning in a given project, administrators, resource personnel, university students, or teachers can be asked to be available. Parents and other community members often enjoy volunteering at library centers. In primary library centers, a parent, adult, or student leader frequently assists with each group, allowing the classroom teacher flexibility to rotate among the groups for expert help and observations.

Evaluation in library centers is ongoing and continuous and is done by both the learners and the instructors. A variety of assessment tools are used, from observation checklists, coaching and discussion, presentations, and celebrations to formal checklists filled out by student and teacher.

Library centers are based on an approximate class size of 30, with 4 to 5 students in each group. Therefore, the teacher-librarian usually needs to make five copies of each center instruction card. The library centers in this book have been designed to be portable because the school library plays host to multiple groups, classes, and other activities throughout the day. Library center instructions and materials are adapted for today's learners and can be printed on colorful, laminated cards. Materials and resources are placed into boxes, plastic buckets, or bins, depending upon what is needed and available. Students, especially those in upper elementary levels, bring their own folders and supplies. Each library center in this book lists the "Materials Needed" as well as "Method," that is, suggestions for implementation.

Library centers make the school library an active, exciting place to be for teachers and students, involved together in the exploration of resource-based learning.

Material in a center

ABC BEARS

Chapter One

The focus of beginning library centers is the alphabet. While these library centers are occurring in the library, primary students can be studying an alphabet theme in the classroom. Alphabet literature from the library collection enhances the units in the classrooms. Often the centers are used partway through the year, when teachers feel the students are ready to use alphabetization skills to find books more independently in the library. Teachers then reserve the library for 45 minutes each day for one week to complete the five centers. Volunteers are organized ahead of time so that all centers have an adult helper; the teacher-librarian is most often involved in instruction at the catalog center.

ABC BEARS 1

Materials Needed

- ABC Bears 1 direction cards. Make a copy of figure 1.1, page 2, for each group to create these cards
- Thirty 8" x 5.5" cards using six different colors of construction paper. Each card names an author of one of the picture books in your collection; underline the first letter of the last name, for example, Frank Asch, Pat Hutchins, Ezra Jack Keats. (See fig. 1.2, p. 3.)

Method

The large cards clearly identify each author's section on the easy book shelves. Because some books may be out on loan and this may be the students' first attempt to find books on the shelves on their own, the cards can be placed close to the author's section. Students who complete placing one set of cards should be encouraged to go on to a second set.

Figure 1.1

From *Library Centers*. © 1997 Judith A. Sykes. Libraries Unlimited. (800) 237-6124.

Figure 1.2

Frank <u>A</u>sch

John <u>B</u>urningham

From *Library Centers.* © 1997 Judith A. Sykes. Libraries Unlimited. (800) 237-6124.

ABC BEARS 2

Materials Needed

- ABC Bears 2 direction cards. (See fig.1.3, p. 5.)
- Seven sets of 4" x 5" cards with 10 cards in each set. Cards use authors' names by first- or second-letter alphabetization based on the library's collection; for example, set one: Frank Asch, Mitsumasa Anno, Martha Alexander; set two: Briggs, Brown, Broeder. (See fig. 1.4, p. 6.)
- A selection of primary magazines such as *Chickadee, Sesame Street, My Big Back Yard.*

Method

Students choose a card set, spread it out on the floor or table, and put the cards in the correct alphabetical order. They should then trade card sets, shuffle them, and try to do each set. If time permits, they may browse through the magazines.

ABC BEARS 3

Materials Needed

- ABC Bears 3 direction cards. (See fig. 1.5, p. 7.)
- Six sets of five word card strips, with each set made from a different color of construction paper. (See fig. 1.6, p. 8.) The word sets should match words in primary dictionaries from your collection.
- Paper and pencils.

Method

With their adult helper, students find the words in the dictionaries and mark the places with the strips. They may then trade dictionaries to do extra sets. If there is additional time, they may list or illustrate some favorite words.

Figure 1.3

From *Library Centers*. ⊃ 1997 Judith A. Sykes. Libraries Unlimited. (800) 237-6124.

Figure 1.4

Frank Asch

Mitsumasa Anno

Martha Alexander

Aliki

From *Library Centers*. © 1997 Judith A. Sykes. Libraries Unlimited. (800) 237-6124.

Figure 1.5

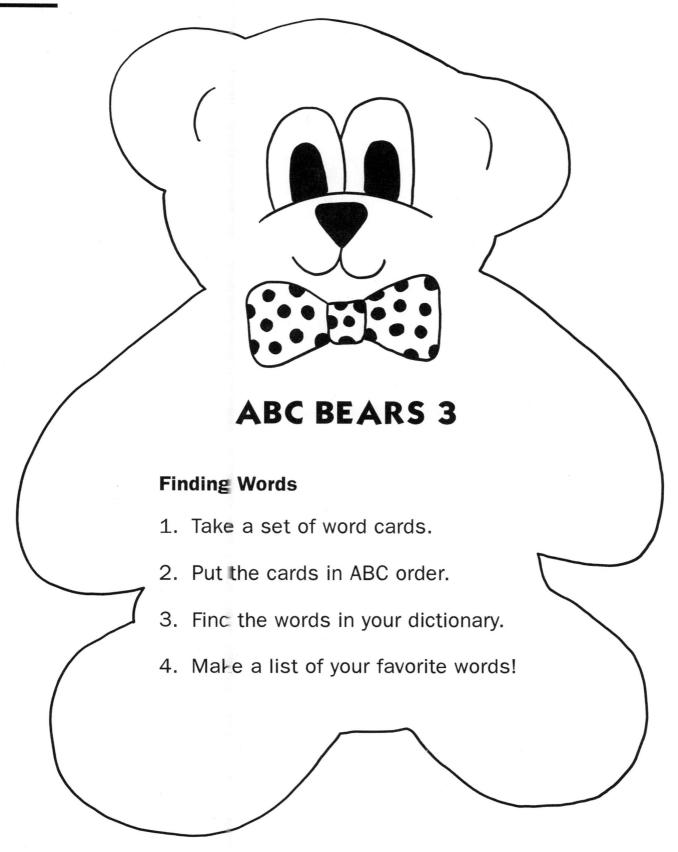

ABC BEARS 3

Finding Words

1. Take a set of word cards.

2. Put the cards in ABC order.

3. Find the words in your dictionary.

4. Make a list of your favorite words!

From *Library Centers*. © 1997 Judith A. Sykes. Libraries Unlimited. (800) 237-6124.

Figure 1.6

farm	pencil	lion	zebra
Golden Picture Dictionary	Golden Picture Dictionary	Golden Picture Dictionary	Golden Picture Dictionary

ABC BEARS 4

Materials Needed

- ABC Bears 4 direction cards. (See fig. 1.7, p. 10.)
- Enough 6" x 8" squares of blank, white, heavy paper so that each student can create a catalog card. (See fig. 1.8, p. 11.)
- Pencils.

Method

Tell the students that the first way to find books in either the card or electronic catalog is by an author's last name. They practice the concept by making an author card using their own last names and stories they are writing or would like to write. Take students to the card catalog and have them find the drawer that matches their last name. If your catalog is electronic, let them type their last names into the computer. Show them examples of favorite authors; point out the call numbers and show them where to find that author's books on the shelf. Some students will want to look up other authors; other students will want to return to their stories.

ABC BEARS 5

Materials Needed

- ABC Bears 5 direction cards. (See fig. 1.9, p. 12.)
- Two worksheets, one with a list of eight picture book authors and titles and the other with a blank list for gluing. (See figs. 1.10 and 1.11, pp. 13 and 14.)
- Scissors and glue.
- Books from your collection that match the worksheet list.

Method

Students practice alphabetizing by creating a bibliography. Once they have cut out the sections, have them arrange the strips alphabetically; check their work before they glue the strips onto the blank paper. The students may then enjoy the book selection; perhaps an adult at the center could read to the students.

Figure 1.7

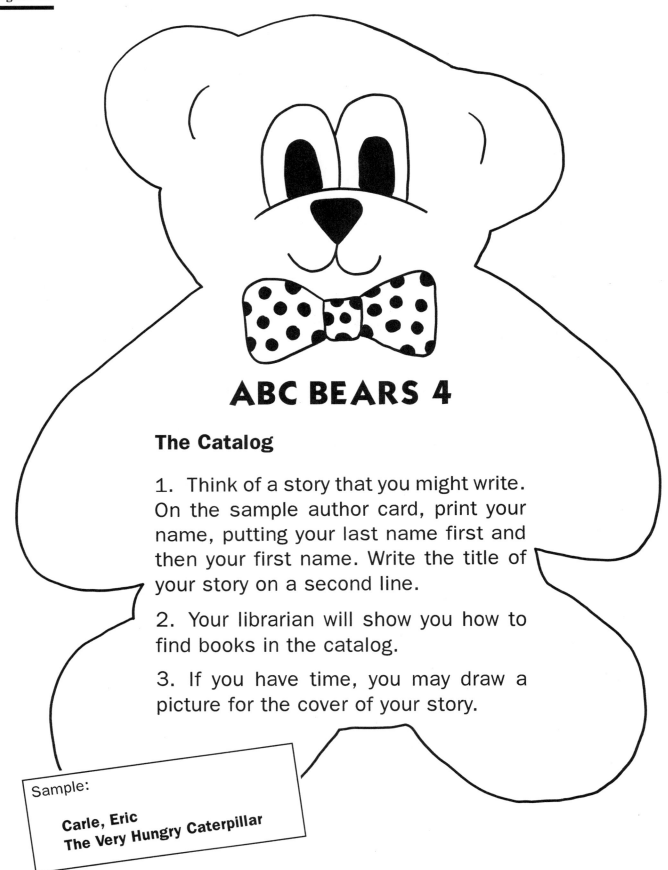

ABC BEARS 4

The Catalog

1. Think of a story that you might write. On the sample author card, print your name, putting your last name first and then your first name. Write the title of your story on a second line.

2. Your librarian will show you how to find books in the catalog.

3. If you have time, you may draw a picture for the cover of your story.

Sample:

Carle, Eric
The Very Hungry Caterpillar

10 From *Library Centers*. © 1997 Judith A. Sykes. Libraries Unlimited. (800) 237-6124.

Figure 1.8

Sykes, Judy
The Skates

From *Library Centers*. © 1997 Judith A. Sykes. Libraries Unlimited. (800) 237-6124.

Figure 1.9

ABC BEARS 5

Bibliography

1. Cut the "book spines" apart.

2. Glue the "spines" onto the shelf page in ABC order by the authors' last names.

3. Enjoy a book!

From *Library Centers*. © 1997 Judith A. Sykes. Libraries Unlimited. (800) 237-6124.

Figure 1.10

HUTCHINS, Pat
Rosie's Walk

ZION, Gene
Harry the Dirty Dog

WILDSMITH, Brian
Bear's Adventure

LIONNI, Leo
Alexander and the Wind-up Mouse

KRAUS, Robert
Whose Mouse Are You?

DUVOISIN, Roger
Veronica

ALEXANDER, Martha
Blackboard Bear

BURNINGHAM, John
Mr. Gumpy's Motorcar

Figure 1.11

ABC BOOKWORMS

Chapter Two

These centers reinforce alphabetizing and library skills for upper primary students and can be used in conjunction with a project during which students write their own alphabet books. The alphabet books from the library collection are presented in a booktalk and circulated to classrooms to serve as examples and to facilitate writing. Students bring drafts of their own alphabet books to the library to work on as they complete the centers. Students rotate through the six centers during the first part of the year. This requires eight one-hour blocks per class: the first to hear a booktalk on the alphabet books and encourage the writing project, the next six for the centers, and the last for some follow-up time for sharing the students' alphabet books. It is helpful to have a teacher or volunteer for each center, because these author cards present a greater challenge than the "ABC Bears" centers.

ABC BOOKWORMS 1

Materials Needed

- ABC Bookworms 1 direction cards. (See fig. 2.1, p. 16.)
- Thirty-six 8.5" x 5.5" cards with names of picture book authors printed clearly. Underline the first letter of each author's last name to cue students. (See fig. 2.2, p. 17.) Choose different and more challenging authors than the ones you used for the "ABC Bears" center.

Method

Students first alphabetize their cards; then they try to locate books by the named author and mark them with the large cards. Encourage as much independence as possible; have students work as teams, checking each other's work and trading card sets.

15

Figure 2.1

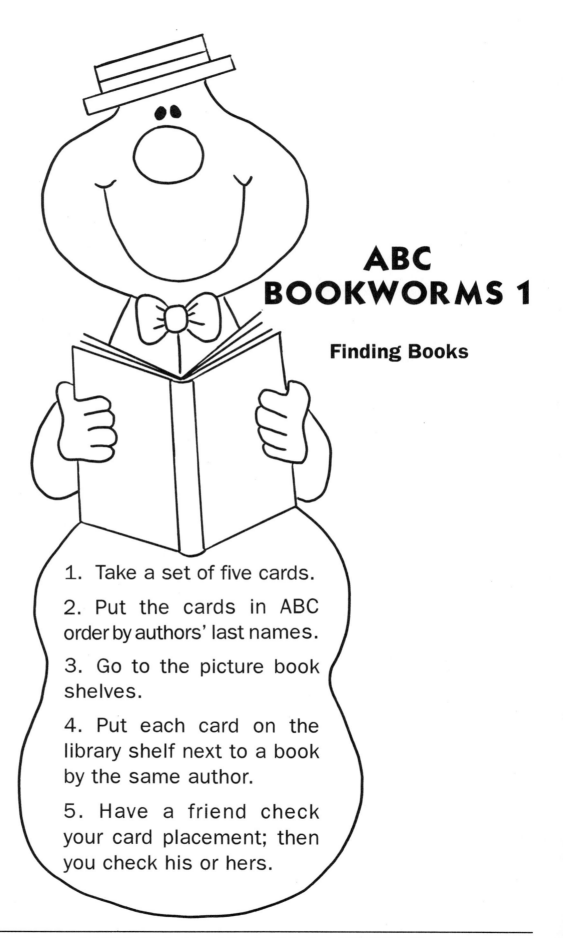

From *Library Centers*. © 1997 Judith A. Sykes. Libraries Unlimited. (800) 237-6124.

Figure 2.2

Marc Brown

James Marshall

From *Library Centers.* © 1997 Judith A. Sykes. Libraries Unlimited. (800) 237-6124.

17

ABC BOOKWORMS 2

Materials Needed

- ABC Bookworms 2 direction cards. (See fig. 2.3, p. 19.)
- Blank paper.
- Donated catalogs for cutting up.
- Scissors, glue, pencils.
- Easy dictionaries.

Method

Helpers will want to ensure that students pace their time in looking through catalogs, cutting, and alphabetizing. It is always wise for the student to have a friend or adult helper check the alphabetizing prior to gluing. Encourage use of the dictionaries for labelling.

ABC BOOKWORMS 3

Materials Needed

- ABC Bookworms 3 direction cards. (See fig. 2.4, p. 20.)
- Six sets of five words each on 4" x 5" cards, each made of a different color of construction paper. (See fig. 2.5, p. 21.) Words should come from current classroom projects or lists.
- Five easy dictionaries.

Method

Before students begin this project, the helper at the library center should give a few beginning dictionary tips to help them locate words faster. The tips might include finding the center of the alphabet, using guide words, and looking at second and third letters. Students should try to complete three sets.

Figure 2.3

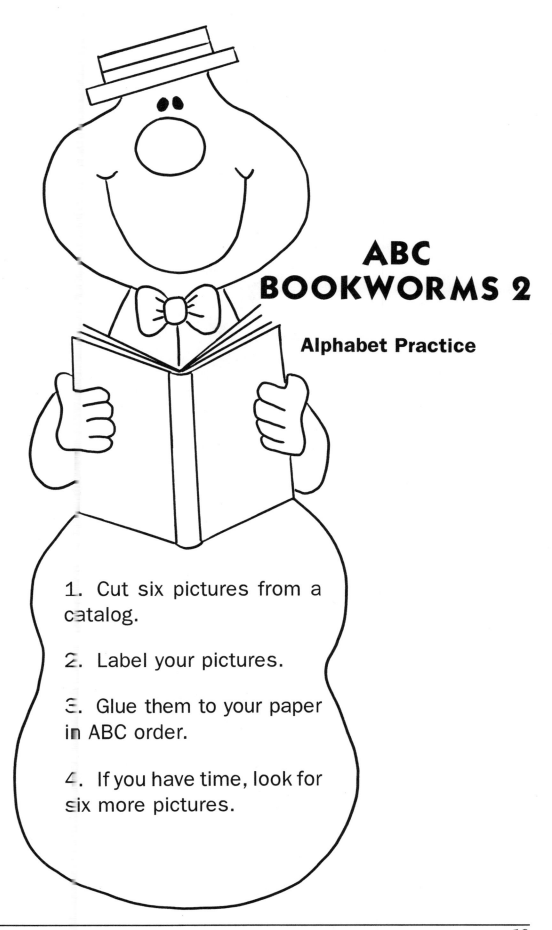

From *Library Centers.* © 1997 Judith A. Sykes. Libraries Unlimited. (800) 237-6124.

Figure 2.4

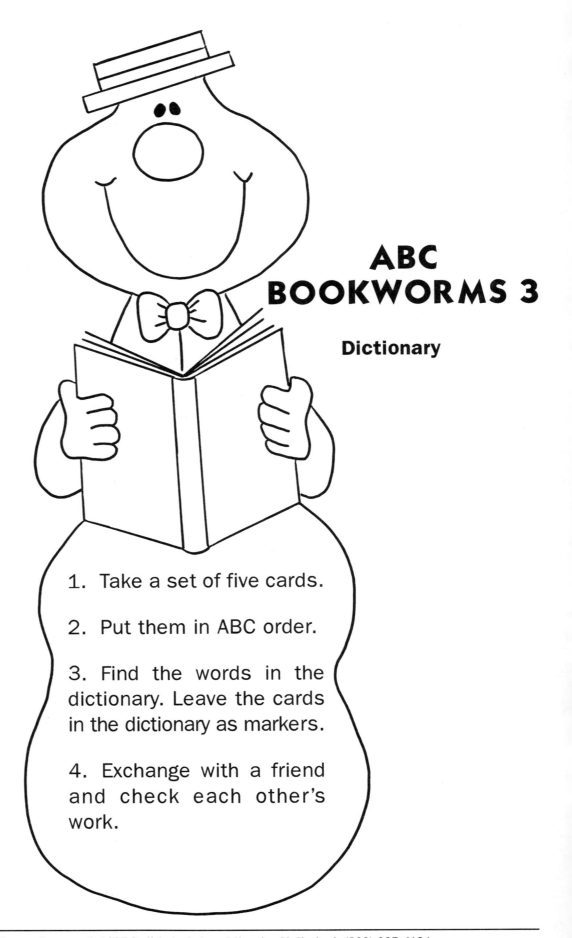

ABC BOOKWORMS 3

Dictionary

1. Take a set of five cards.

2. Put them in ABC order.

3. Find the words in the dictionary. Leave the cards in the dictionary as markers.

4. Exchange with a friend and check each other's work.

Figure 2.5

sick

friend

heavy

game

From *Library Centers* © 1997 Judith A. Sykes. Libraries Unlimited. (800) 237-6124.

ABC BOOKWORMS 4

Materials Needed
- ABC Bookworms 4 direction cards. (See fig. 2.6, p. 23.)
- Blank library (index-type) cards; enough for the class.
- Pencils.
- A selection of small library cards with a variety of picture book authors' names.

Method

Whether you have an electronic catalog or a card catalog, the method is similar. The basic library card or electronic record begins with the author's last name followed by the book title. If you have both a card catalog and an electronic catalog, have the students do the activity in both places. Students will type their last names or the authors' last names into the electronic catalog. Point out the connection to the actual library shelves via call numbers.

ABC BOOKWORMS 5

Materials Needed
- ABC Bookworms 5 direction cards. (See fig. 2.7, p. 24.)
- Worksheet naming 10 picture books, each listed with author and title. (See fig. 2.8, p. 25.)
- Blank worksheet for pasting. (See fig. 2.9, p. 26.)
- Scissors, glue.
- Books that match worksheet titles.

Method

Students should be encouraged to have peers check their work before gluing. They may read the books as individuals or teams when the activity is complete.

Figure 2.6

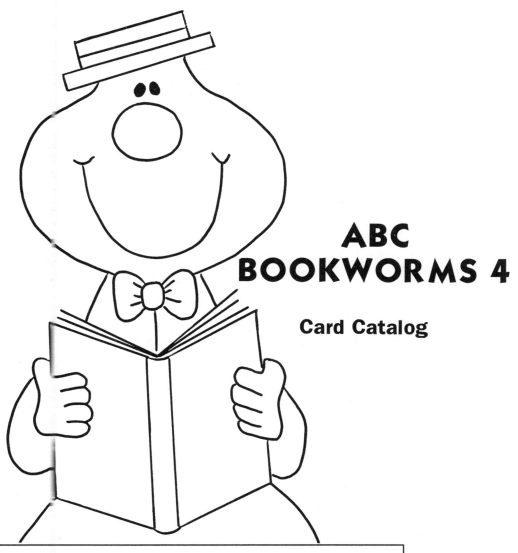

ABC BOOKWORMS 4

Card Catalog

1. Fill in your catalog card with your name, putting your last name first and then your first name. On a separate line, fill in the title of your ABC book.

2. Put your group's cards in ABC order. Do this as a team.

3. When you are done, go to the author entry of your catalog. See if you can find where your name would go!

4. Have a friend or helper check your work.

5. Select an author card from the tray and try to find that author in the catalog.

From *Library Centers.* © 1997 Judith A. Sykes. Libraries Unlimited. (800) 237-6124.

Figure 2.7

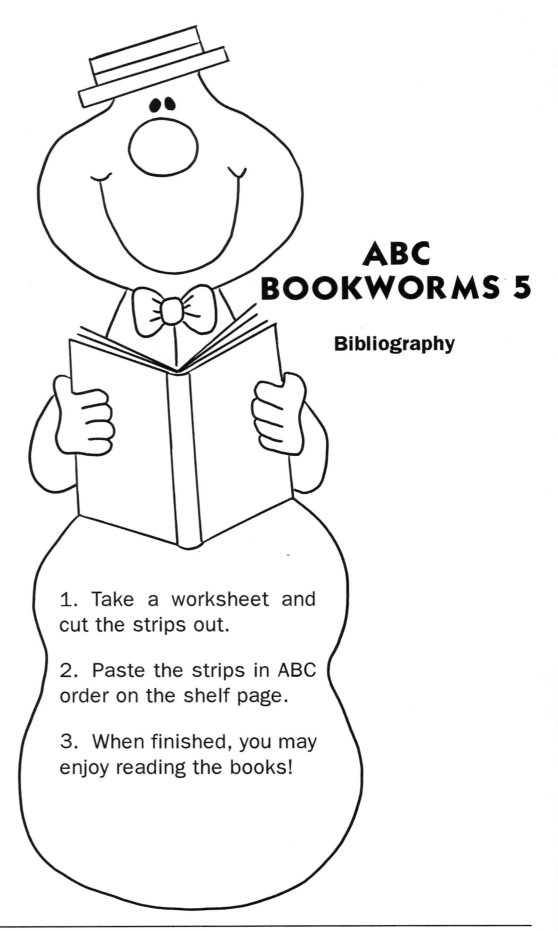

ABC BOOKWORMS 5

Bibliography

1. Take a worksheet and cut the strips out.

2. Paste the strips in ABC order on the shelf page.

3. When finished, you may enjoy reading the books!

24   From *Library Centers*. © 1997 Judith A. Sykes. Libraries Unlimited. (800) 237-6124.

Figure 2.8

LOBEL, Arnold
Frog and Toad Are Friends

HOFF, Syd
Danny and the Dinosaur

PEET, Bill
Fly Homer Fly

KESSLER, Ethel
The Sweeneys from 9D

SCARRY, Richard
Find Your ABC's

GRAMATKY, Hardie
Little Toot

BENCHLEY, Nathaniel
Red Fox and His Canoe

McCLOSKEY, Robert
Make Way for Ducklings

ZOLOTOW, Charlotte
A Tiger for Timothy

DePAOLA, Tomie
Little Grunt and the Big Egg

From *Library Centers.* © 1997 Judith A. Sykes. Libraries Unlimited. (800) 237-6124.

Figure 2.9

From *Library Centers*. © 1997 Judith A. Sykes. Libraries Unlimited. (800) 237-6124.

ABC BOOKWORMS 6

Materials Needed

- ABC Bookworms 6 direction cards. (See fig. 2.10, p. 28.)
- Six sets of 10 4" x 5' cards, in a variety of colors, using authors' last names that begin with the same letter. For example, Brown, Bright, Berenstain, Burningham; Seuss, Sharmat, Silverstein.

Method

Students may spread their cards out on the carpet or tables to make alphabetizing easier. This level of library center builds their skills in alphabetizing to the second or third letter. They should be encouraged to do all sets.

Figure 2.10

ABC BOOKWORMS 6

Alphabetizing to Next Letter

1. Take a set of 10 colored author cards.

2. Put the cards in ABC order by the authors' last names.

3. Check your cards with a friend or helper.

4. Go on to another set of cards.

From *Library Centers*. © 1997 Judith A. Sykes. Libraries Unlimited. (800) 237-6124.

BRIDGE BOOKS

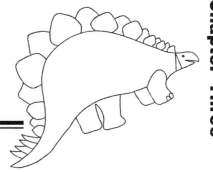

Chapter Three

In these centers students practice alphabetizing, cataloging, and library location skills while discovering authors who "bridge" easy and junior fiction. This includes beginning chapter books as well as more challenging "easy" books such as Chris Van Allsburg's *Jumanji*. Each student chooses a book and shares it with peers throughout the term via a continuing series of student booktalks. The centers are introduced early in the year, often to third graders, and require six hour-long sessions per class, with follow-up time for student booktalks. As always, volunteers are helpful for assistance at these centers.

BRIDGE BOOKS 1

Materials Needed
- Bridge Books 1 direction cards. (See fig. 3.1, p. 30.)
- Discarded magazines and catalogs.
- Paper, scissors, glue, pencils.
- Dictionaries.

Method

Encourage students to find six pictures and provide assistance if they cannot quickly locate appropriate pictures for their chosen letter. They should be encouraged to use the dictionaries to help them spell the words when they label their pictures.

29

Figure 3.1

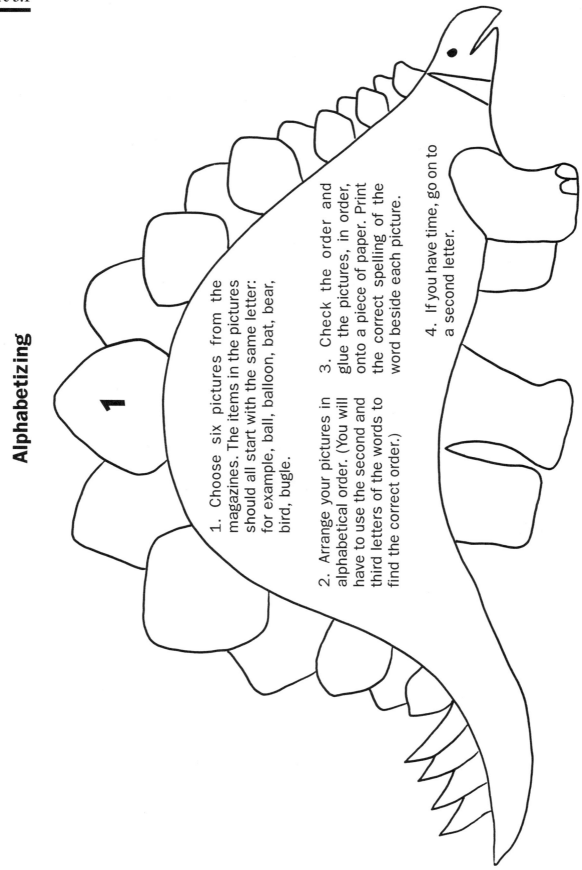

Alphabetizing

1

1. Choose six pictures from the magazines. The items in the pictures should all start with the same letter: for example, ball, balloon, bat, bear, bird, bugle.

2. Arrange your pictures in alphabetical order. (You will have to use the second and third letters of the words to find the correct order.)

3. Check the order and glue the pictures, in order, onto a piece of paper. Print the correct spelling of the word beside each picture.

4. If you have time, go on to a second letter.

From *Library Centers.* © 1997 Judith A. Sykes. Libraries Unlimited. (800) 237-6124.

BRIDGE BOOKS 2

Materials Needed

- Bridge Books 2 direction cards. (See fig. 3.2, p. 32.)
- Set of 20 3" x 4" word cards with words based on current classroom study. (For instance, for a class doing a natural history unit, words might include *salamander, decay, reed, aquarium,* and so on. See fig. 3.3, p. 33.)
- Five junior dictionaries, third- to fourth-grade level.
- Paper, pencils.

Method

Instruct students to open the dictionaries to the letter *m*. Point out that *m* is in the middle of the alphabet. Ask students if *s* is before or after *m*. Ask where other letters are found in relation to *m*; then close the dictionaries. Show students one word card and ask them to estimate where the word would be found. Open the dictionary to their estimation. Have them note how far they are from the letter they were looking for. Once you find the word, read the entry and discuss the main definition. Repeat with other examples.

Students may then choose their own words and continue the activity.

BRIDGE BOOKS 3

Materials Needed

- Bridge Books 3 direction cards. (See fig. 3.4, p. 34.)
- Large size art paper (8.5" x 14").
- Pencils, crayons, pastels, felt-tip pens and markers, or paints.
- Five or six excellent (Caldecott or other award-winning) picture books that demonstrate a variety of illustration styles, such as watercolor, oil paint, collage, ink, print/sponge painting, kaleidoscope, and others.

Method

A library center helper can lead a discussion about the parts of a book and illustration style at any point during the center, or the teacher-librarian can facilitate such a discussion before the center begins, either in the library or in the classroom. Students should first study the cover, both back and front. Point out the title page inside, explaining that the *publisher* is the company that had the book printed. On the back of the title page is the year of publication and the copyright notice; point out that no one else can copy that book without permission. Discuss the various styles of illustration demonstrated by the chosen books. Encourage students to begin their own book jackets. Check with the teacher so you can plan these centers around current story-writing activities being done in the classroom.

31

Figure 3.2

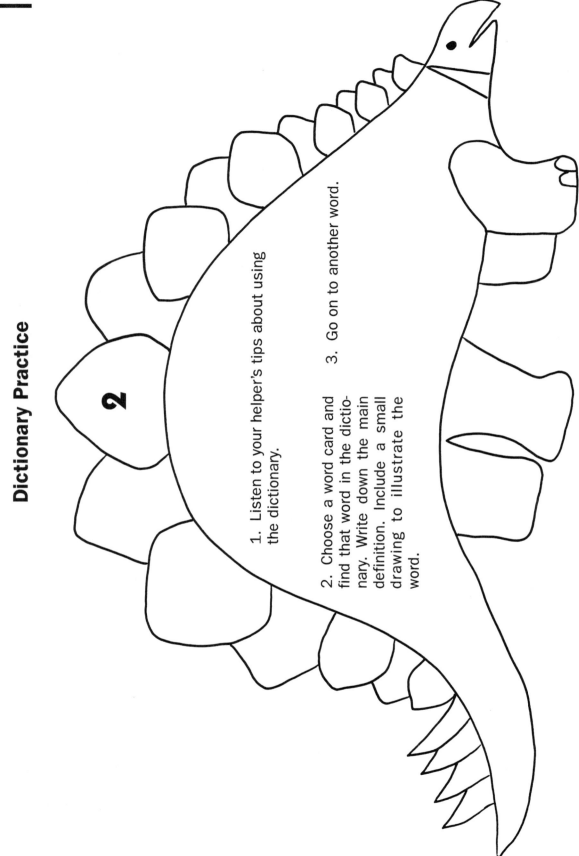

32   From *Library Centers*. © 1997 Judith A. Sykes. Libraries Unlimited. (800) 237-6124.

Figure 3.3

control	unique
oboe	slender
salamander	assist
reed	principal
decay	mood
employ	malt

From *Library Centers* © 1997 Judith A. Sykes. Libraries Unlimited. (800) 237-6124.

Figure 3.4

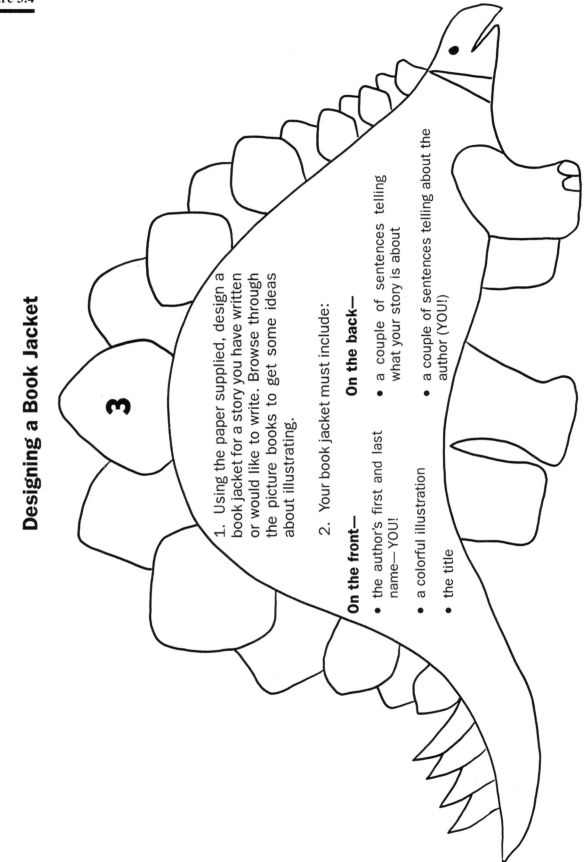

Designing a Book Jacket

3

1. Using the paper supplied, design a book jacket for a story you have written or would like to write. Browse through the picture books to get some ideas about illustrating.

2. Your book jacket must include:

On the front—
- the author's first and last name—YOU!
- a colorful illustration
- the title

On the back—
- a couple of sentences telling what your story is about
- a couple of sentences telling about the author (YOU!)

34   From *Library Centers*. © 1997 Judith A. Sykes. Libraries Unlimited. (800) 237-6124.

BRIDGE BOOKS 4

Materials Needed

- Bridge Books 4 direction cards. (See fig. 3.5, p. 36.)
- A selection of 50 or 60 "bridge" books (easy chapter books or challenging picture books from your collection).

Method

Keep the featured books on a book cart. During center time, have students arrange them in a story corner or large area so that they are surrounded by books!

The teacher or teacher-librarian for this center can demonstrate to the students how to give an effective booktalk by using a favorite bridge book. The booktalk should be about five minutes long and include a short (no longer than one page or paragraph) oral reading of a favorite selection from the book. Assist students in finding books and preparing their own booktalks. Remind them to rehearse reading the selection before they give their booktalk. Parents can assist with this activity and should be specially invited to share the day when their child is presenting a booktalk.

Before students browse through the selection of books, share tips about choosing books with them, such as reading the first page, checking the book jacket, checking the book's length, and so on.

BRIDGE BOOKS 5

Materials Needed

- Bridge Books 5 direction cards. (See fig. 3.6, p. 37.)
- Paper, pencils, rulers.
- Six sets of index cards with lists of five "bridge" authors, such as

    Hurwitz, Johanna   Park, Barbara
    Howe, James   Peet, Bill
    Munsch, Robert

Method

The helper at this center is often the teacher-librarian. He or she coaches the students through the steps of using the catalog record, assisting and checking their work. Students may work either at a card catalog or by typing author searches into an electronic catalog. Students may work in pairs or small groups.

Figure 3.5

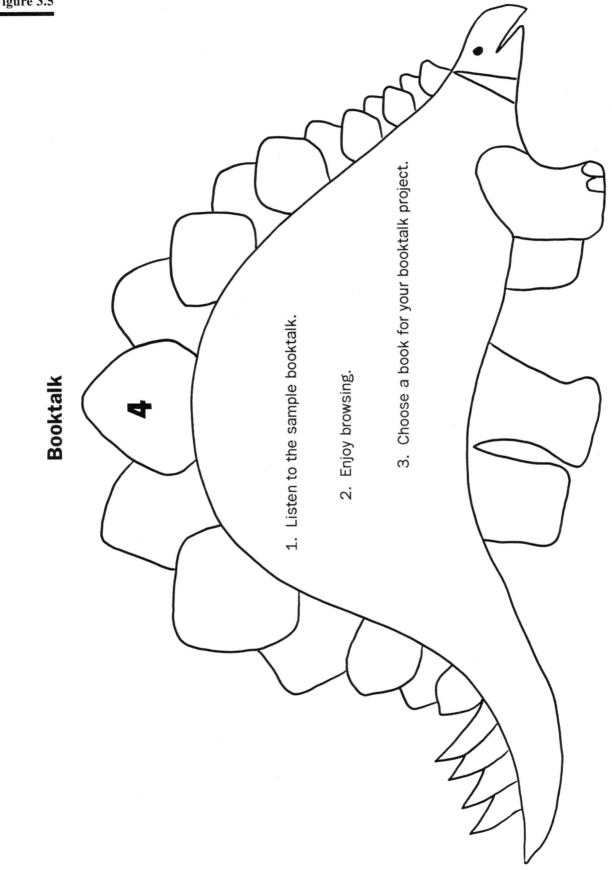

Figure 3.6

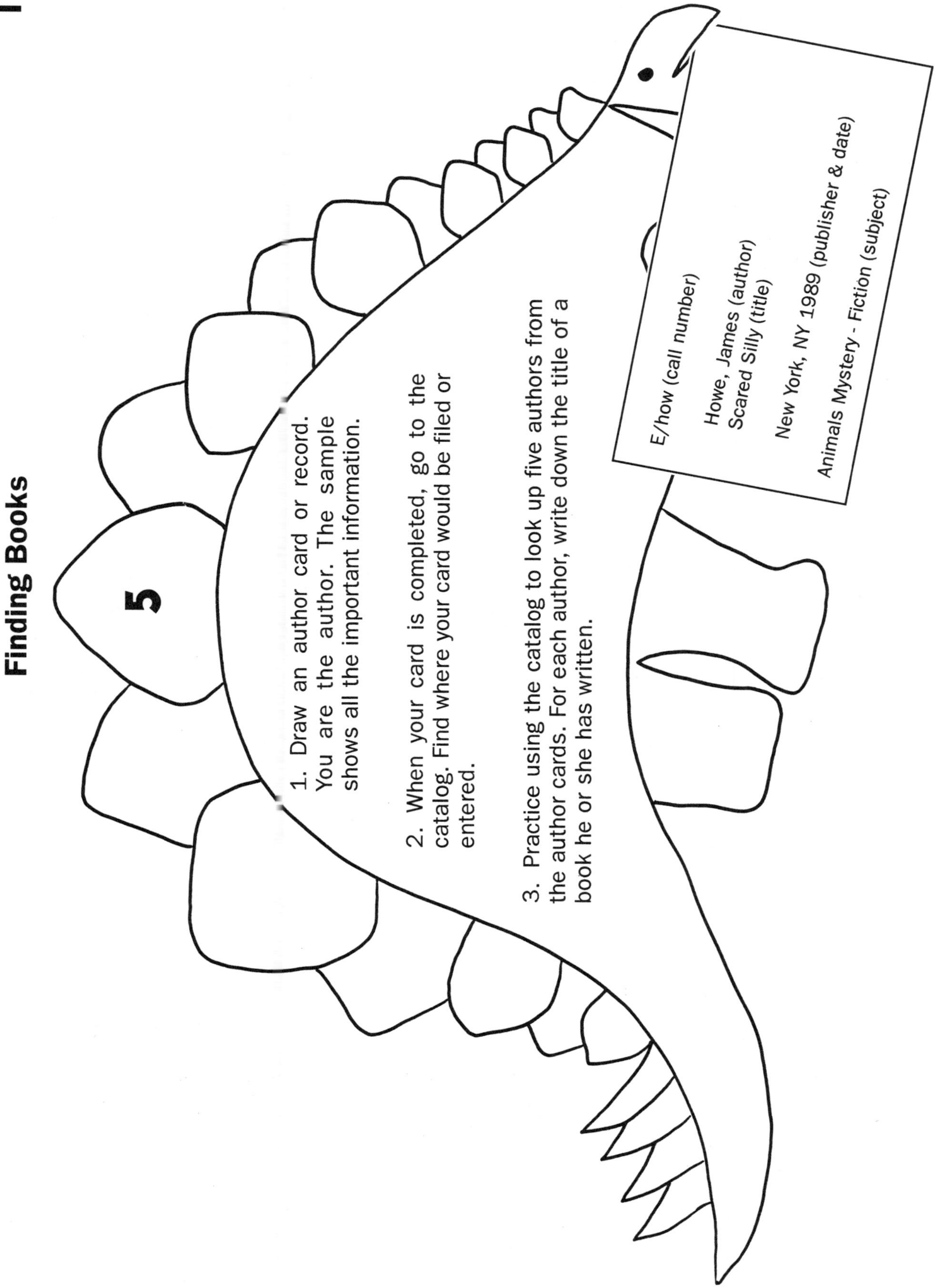

Finding Books

5

1. Draw an author card or record. You are the author. The sample shows all the important information.

2. When your card is completed, go to the catalog. Find where your card would be filed or entered.

3. Practice using the catalog to look up five authors from the author cards. For each author, write down the title of a book he or she has written.

E/how (call number)

Howe, James (author)
Scared Silly (title)

New York, NY 1989 (publisher & date)

Animals Mystery - Fiction (subject)

BRIDGE BOOKS 6

Materials Needed

- Bridge Books 6 direction cards. (See fig. 3.7, p. 39.)
- Fifty author cards. Make the cards out of construction paper and cut them into strips the size of a ruler to resemble a shelf marker. The authors on the strips should be those from your collection who write both easy and beginning junior fiction, such as Peggy Parish and James Howe.

Method

Have the students alternate activities—finding books on the shelves or finding catalog entries—depending on the amount of room at your catalog or the number of electronic terminals you have. A group of five or six students could be divided for these activities.

Figure 3.7

Fiction on the Shelf

1. Choose five author cards. Put them in alphabetical order by the authors' last names.

2. Find books on either the junior or easy shelves by that author. Use the cards to mark the place. Have your friend or helper check your work.

3. Use the card catalog to help you find books by the author in the library.

From *Library Centers.* © 1997 Judith A. Sykes. Libraries Unlimited. (800) 237-6124.

JUNIOR AUTHORS

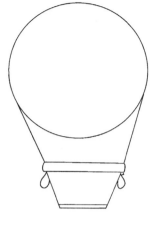

Chapter Four

These centers can be taught in conjunction with a novel study or reader's workshop, or as an introduction to classic children's authors for beginning upper elementary students. Six hours per class are needed, usually in the first part of the year, following some preparation in the classroom. A more independent, cooperative approach to group interactions should be discussed with the students. Students should also be prepared to rotate into and out of appropriate group roles, such as reader, recorder, and so on.

At this level, only three of the six centers need direct adult or volunteer assistance, and even those for only some of the time. The teacher and teacher-librarian act as coaches or facilitators. Students should read the center cards to organize their tasks. They need to learn to ask other group members for assistance before they seek out an adult helper or teacher.

JUNIOR AUTHORS 1

Materials Needed

- Junior Authors 1 direction cards. (See fig. 4.1, p. 42.)
- Fifty ruler-sized strips of laminated colored card stock with authors' names to match fourth-grade-appropriate books from your collection (for example, A. A. Milne, C. S. Lewis, Johanna Hurwitz, Donald Sobol, Beverly Cleary).
- Paper, pencils, rulers.

Method

Students should be able to accomplish this activity independently, although some students will need to be reminded where the junior books are located and how they are alphabetized. As the teachers circulate, they may wish to check periodically to see that students are successfully locating the authors.

41

Figure 4.1

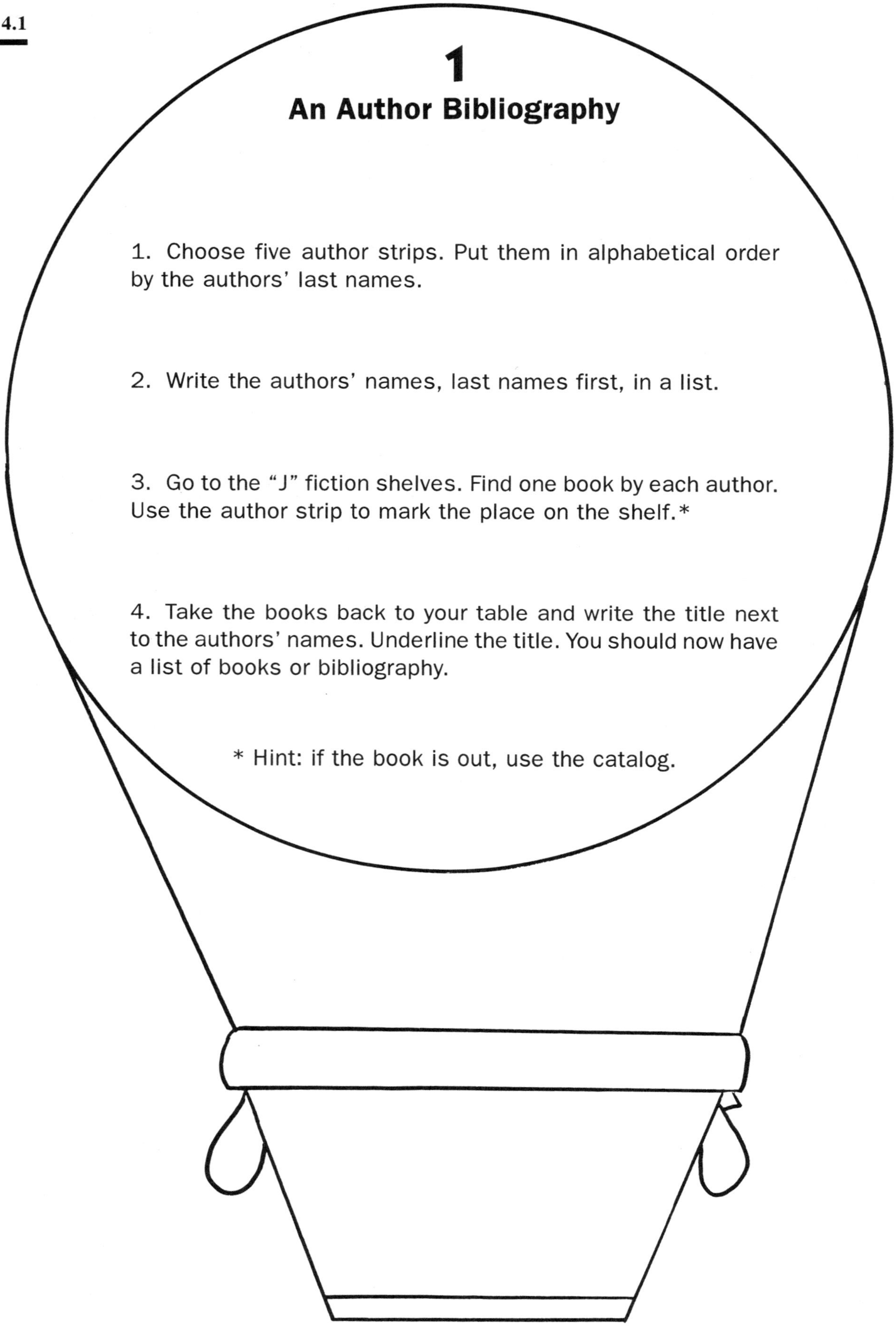

1
An Author Bibliography

1. Choose five author strips. Put them in alphabetical order by the authors' last names.

2. Write the authors' names, last names first, in a list.

3. Go to the "J" fiction shelves. Find one book by each author. Use the author strip to mark the place on the shelf.*

4. Take the books back to your table and write the title next to the authors' names. Underline the title. You should now have a list of books or bibliography.

* Hint: if the book is out, use the catalog.

From *Library Centers*. © 1997 Judith A. Sykes. Libraries Unlimited. (800) 237-6124.

JUNIOR AUTHORS 2

Materials Needed

- Junior Authors 2 direction cards. (See fig. 4.2, p. 44.)
- Rulers, paper, pencils.

Method

Students should be able to complete the work independently, with the teacher-librarian or helpers making only periodic checks on the group. If you have an automated card catalog, have students do the searches on the computer terminals. Use the examples of authors listed or choose authors from your collection.

JUNIOR AUTHORS 3

Materials Needed

- Junior Authors 3 direction cards. (See fig. 4.3, p. 45.)
- Draft paper, art paper, pencils, colored pencils, crayons, markers, or paints.
- Examples of beautifully illustrated fairy tales or legends from your collection.

Method

The teacher or teacher-librarian should precede these centers with a discussion about setting—what it is and how it is important to a story. Students work independently at this center, with teachers coaching periodically. Encourage students to develop detail and to concentrate on setting—details such as dishes or furniture in a house—and not on drawing characters or actions.

Figure 4.2

2
Finding Books

1. Fill in the information to make your own author card.

2. Go to the catalog. Is there an author with the same last name as yours? Can you find your favorite author?

3. Look up the following authors. Write down one book each author has written. Is the book an easy or a junior book?

Judy Blume   Astrid Lindgren
Beverly Cleary   A. A. Milne
Robert Munsch

4. Look up the following titles to discover who wrote these books: *Owl Moon, Fifteen, Soup and Me.*

5. Choose a subject that you are interested in. Look up a book about that topic. Write down the call number. Go to the bookshelves and see if you can find the book.

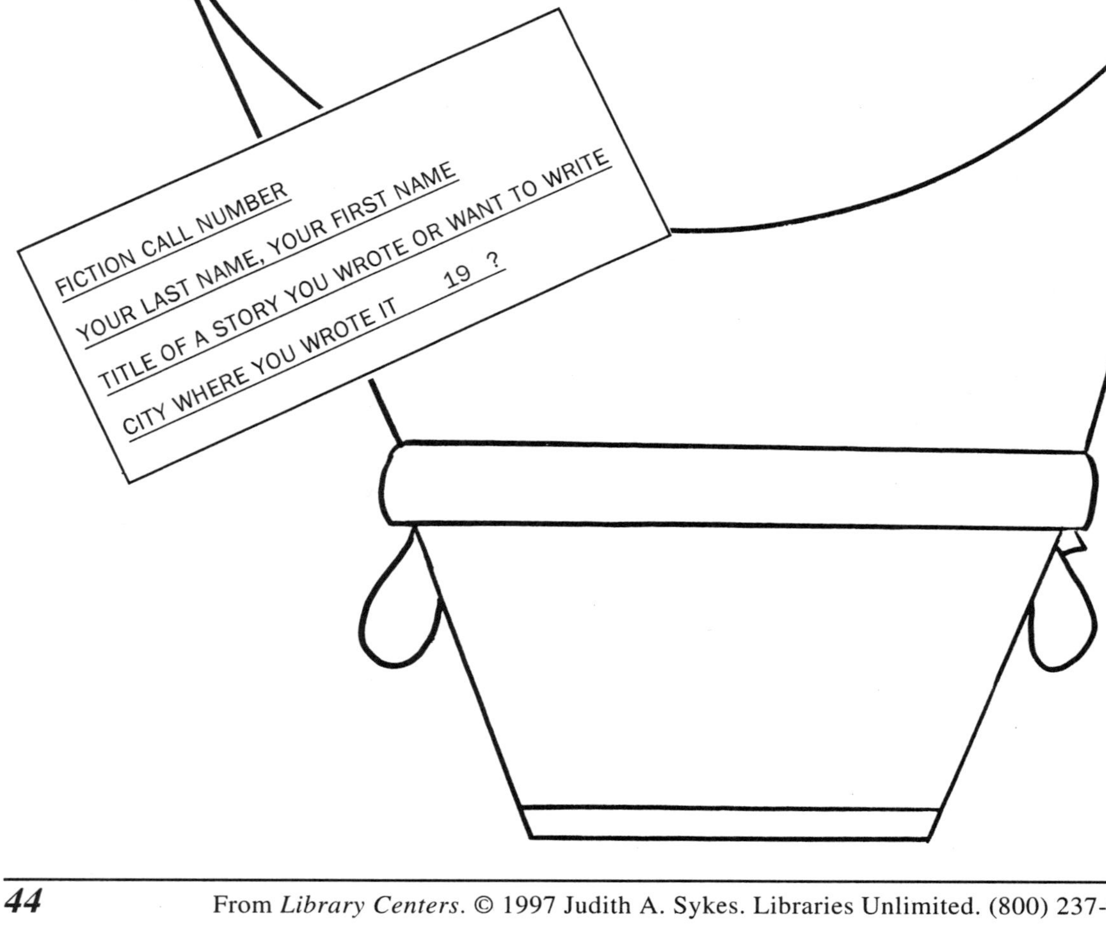

FICTION CALL NUMBER

YOUR LAST NAME, YOUR FIRST NAME

TITLE OF A STORY YOU WROTE OR WANT TO WRITE

CITY WHERE YOU WROTE IT   19 ?

44   From *Library Centers*. © 1997 Judith A. Sykes. Libraries Unlimited. (800) 237-6124.

Figure 4.3

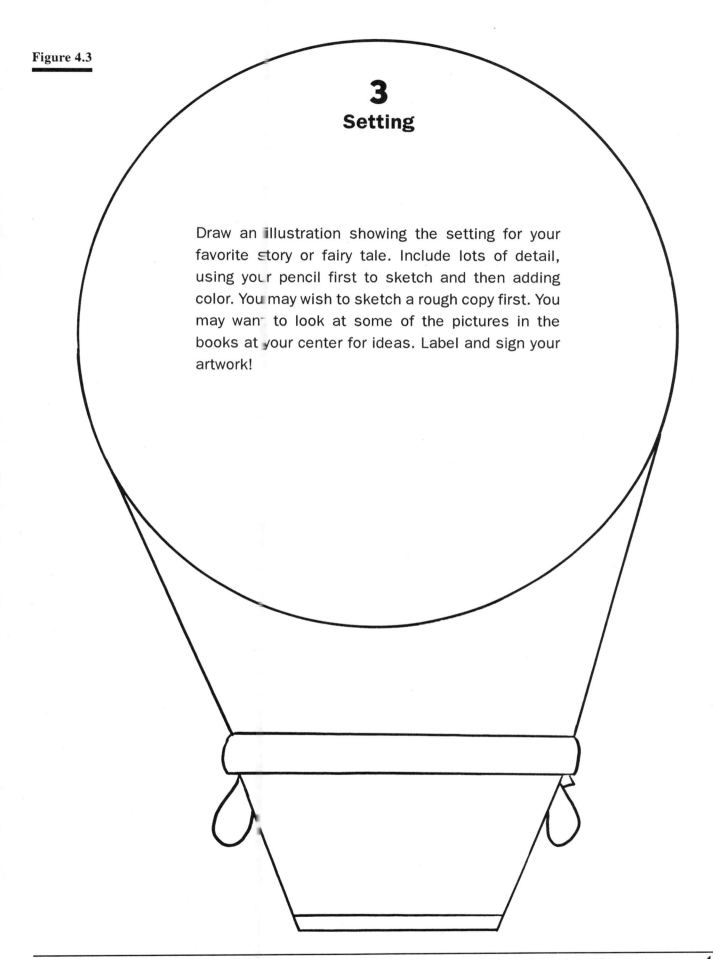

3
Setting

Draw an illustration showing the setting for your favorite story or fairy tale. Include lots of detail, using your pencil first to sketch and then adding color. You may wish to sketch a rough copy first. You may want to look at some of the pictures in the books at your center for ideas. Label and sign your artwork!

From *Library Centers*. © 1997 Judith A. Sykes. Libraries Unlimited. (800) 237-6124.

JUNIOR AUTHORS 4

Materials Needed

- Junior Authors 4 direction cards. (See fig. 4.4, p. 47.)
- A recent volume of *Something About the Author* or a similar author research tool, such as the new CD-ROM "Junior Discovering Authors."
- Notepaper, pencils, word processors if available.

Method

For many students, this is a first introduction to author reference books. The teacher or teacher-librarian should plan on introducing this center and assisting the students in locating the volumes or information about their chosen authors. Choose classic or well-known children's authors for this activity so that students are assured success at finding the information the first time with this type of reference source. If choosing other authors suited to the grade, check to make sure you have information about those authors on hand; your purpose here is to teach students how to use the source. Other methods of researching authors can be introduced later. Once the students have data to work with, the teacher or teacher-librarian can circulate to other centers.

JUNIOR AUTHORS 5

Materials Needed

- Junior Authors 5 direction cards. (See fig. 4.5, p. 48.)
- Five or six small cards with Dewey decimal numbers of popular subjects: 300s, 500s, 600s, 700s, 900s.
- Pencils, 8.5" x 14" poster paper, colored pencils, glue, scissors.
- Magazine discards, especially nature and sports magazines.

Method

The teacher, teacher-librarian, or volunteer may want to check that students have found their Dewey sections and understand the concept of subjects within that number. They sometimes get confused and record titles of books instead of subjects (for instance, in the 500s, plants, dinosaurs, bears). Spelling of the subject words may have to be edited. Encourage peer editing and student dictionary use.

Figure 4.4

4
Author Research

1. Look at the book called *Something About the Author* at your table.

2. Find the author index to locate one of the following authors: Frank L. Baum, Judy Blume, Betsy Byars, Beverly Cleary, Roald Dahl, Charles Dickens, Paul Galdone, C. S. Lewis, Astrid Lindgren, Farley Mowat.

3. In the index, look at the number after the author's name. This is the volume number. Get that volume to read about the author.

4. Answer these questions:
   - What year was the author born?
   - Where was the author born?
   - Is the author still alive? If not, what year did he or she die?
   - What are at least three books that the author has written?

5. Using the information you have discovered, write a paragraph about this author. Write your paragraph on the computer if you have access. Edit your paragraph.

From *Library Centers*. © 1997 Judith A. Sykes. Libraries Unlimited. (800) 237-6124.

Figure 4.5

5
**Favorite
Dewey Decimal Numbers**

1. Choose a Dewey decimal card.

2. Explore! Find the bookshelves with that Dewey number. Look at the kinds of books that have that number. Write down 10 subjects of books that you found in that number.

3. Create a mini-poster about your number. You may either draw your subjects or look through the magazine box to find pictures of your subject to cut out to arrange on your poster. Don't forget to label your pictures.

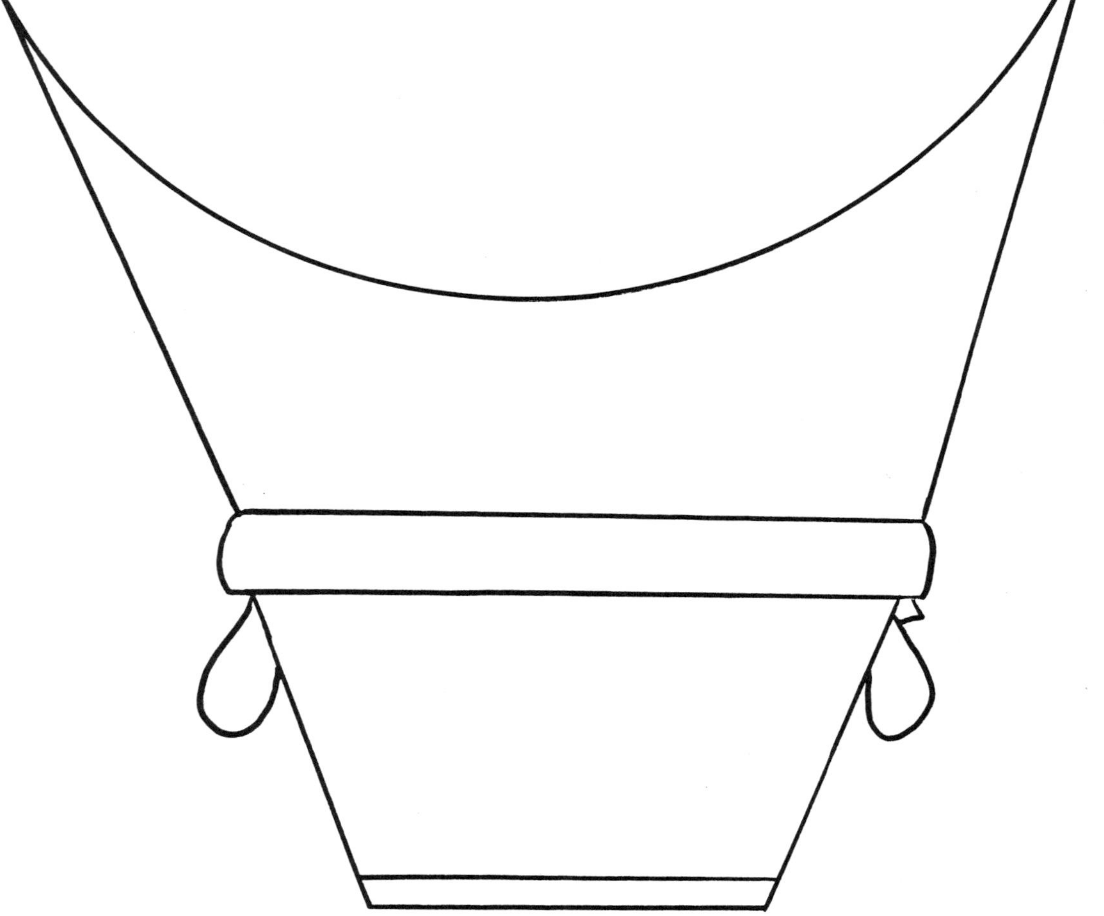

JUNIOR AUTHORS 6

Materials Needed

- Junior Authors 6 direction cards. (See fig. 4.6, p. 50.)
- A blank symbolic map of your library and a legend worksheet. (A sample legend worksheet is shown in fig. 4.7, p. 51.)
- Pencils, crayons, markers.

Method

Students may need some assistance in finding the various items or areas of the library. The teacher or teacher-librarian can rotate to this center to help, or can assign a volunteer to monitor the mapping.

Figure 4.6

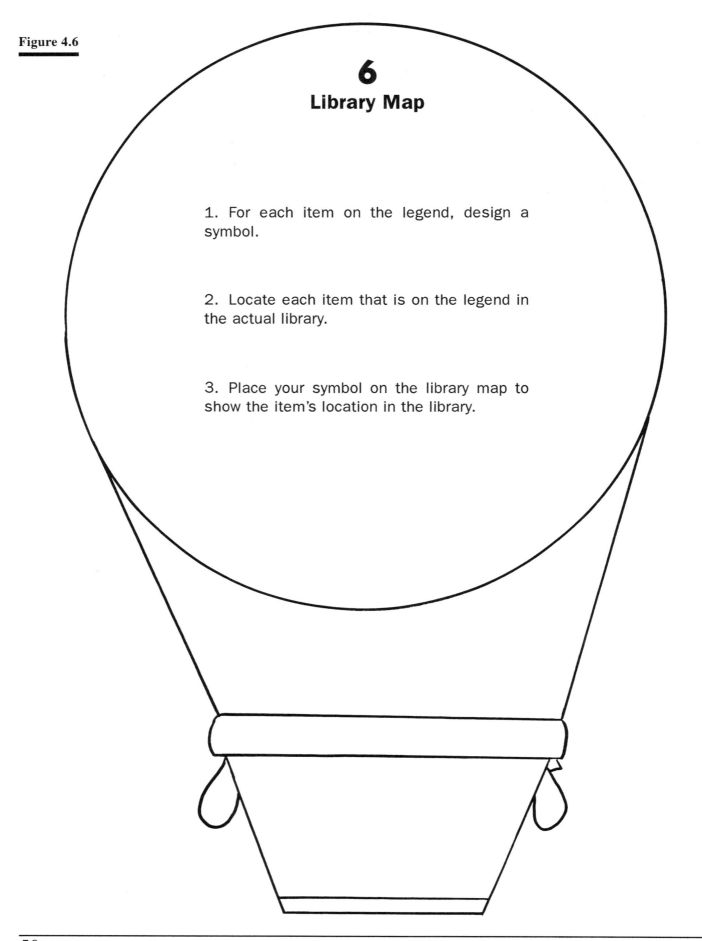

**6
Library Map**

1. For each item on the legend, design a symbol.

2. Locate each item that is on the legend in the actual library.

3. Place your symbol on the library map to show the item's location in the library.

Figure 4.7

6
Library Legend

ITEM	SYMBOL
Easy Fiction	
Easy Non-Fiction	
Junior Fiction	
Junior Non-Fiction	
Reference Books	
Catalog	
Paperbacks	
Check-out Counter	
Magazines	
Picture Files	
CD-ROM Station	
Computers*	

* There may be several computers, so students may have to use their "computer" symbols more than once.

From *Library Centers* © 1997 Judith A. Sykes. Libraries Unlimited. (800) 237-6124.

RATTLING READERS

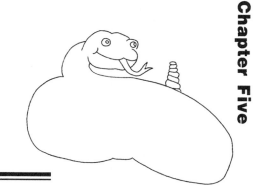

Chapter Five

This next level of library centers can be facilitated by use of the reader's workshop approach, whereby students choose novels they wish to read and study based on a booktalk by the teacher-librarian or the teaching team. Students then read, respond in journals, and prepare projects based on their chosen novels, with teachers and the teacher-librarian sharing groups and guiding them through the process. Using the reader's workshop approach, upper elementary classes can reserve a four-week block in the library, at least two hours per week per class, if the librarian is taking part in the workshop part of the unit. If the teacher-librarian is only taking part in the centers, a full-week block is needed, with an hour per day per class. Alternatively, a month may be set aside during which classes rotate by week at a particular time of the day. An additional couple of hours may be needed for videotaping or presenting author interviews (such as those created in center 3, p. 54). Some of the centers, such as those on setting and character, are designed primarily for independent activity, as the teacher and teacher-librarian will be more needed and will be spending more time assisting at other centers, such as those on author reference or catalog use. Students will need copies of their chosen novels for use at the centers.

An evaluation form has been included with this chapter (see fig. 5.6, p. 62). These forms often accompany student report cards with reflective and anecdotal comments from the students, teachers, and teacher-librarian.

RATTLING READERS 1

Materials Needed

- Rattling Readers 1 direction cards. (See fig. 5.1, p. 55.)
- Fifty ruler-sized strips of construction paper with selected names of junior authors you wish to highlight from your collection (such as Robert Newton Peck, Lois Lowry, Eth Clifford, E. W. Hildick, Judy Blume, and so on).

53

Method

The teacher or teacher-librarian may need to spend a few moments with the group, directing them to the junior bookshelves and helping them find the first book. Tell students to check with the teacher or teacher-librarian on other searches if they can't find the author; sometimes they miss the correct shelf. Other times the books are out, and students can be directed to the card or electronic catalog. Bibliographies may have to be edited.

RATTLING READERS 2

Materials Needed

- Rattling Readers 2 direction cards. (See fig. 5.2, p. 56.)
- Thirty index cards with names of junior authors from your collection.
- Twenty index cards with titles of books from your collection.

Method

Most students will be able to complete the first four activities with minimal, circulating assistance from a teacher or teacher-librarian. Students may need assistance working with the card or electronic catalog.

RATTLING READERS 3

Materials Needed

- Rattling Readers 3 direction cards. (See fig. 5.3, p. 57.)
- Author reference sources, such as *Something About the Author,* "Junior Discovering Authors" CD-ROM, and so on.
- Video camera and blank videotapes for each class. (If video equipment is not available, students can present the interviews live or audiotape them.)

Method

Students may need assistance in locating information about their authors and often require help with script writing. When it is time to videotape interviews, the teacher or teacher-librarian can teach the first pair of students how to use the video camera. That pair can then videotape the second pair and teach them how to use the camera. The second pair then tapes and teaches the third pair, and so on, until the interviews are completed.

Figure 5.1

RATTLING READERS 1

An Author Bibliography

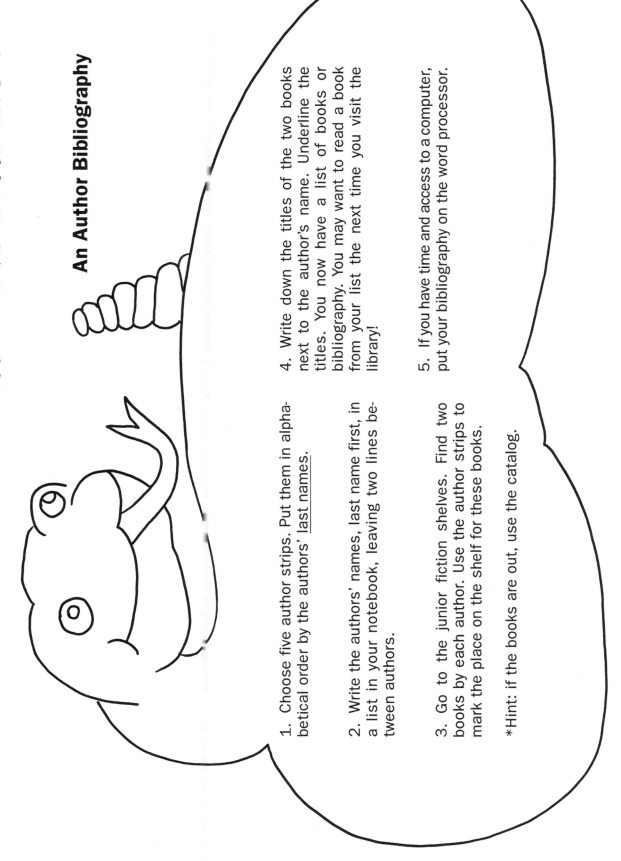

1. Choose five author strips. Put them in alphabetical order by the authors' last names.

2. Write the authors' names, last name first, in a list in your notebook, leaving two lines between authors.

3. Go to the junior fiction shelves. Find two books by each author. Use the author strips to mark the place on the shelf for these books.

4. Write down the titles of the two books next to the author's name. Underline the titles. You now have a list of books or bibliography. You may want to read a book from your list the next time you visit the library!

5. If you have time and access to a computer, put your bibliography on the word processor.

*Hint: if the books are out, use the catalog.

From *Library Centers* © 1997 Judith A. Sykes. Libraries Unlimited. (800) 237-6124.   55

Figure 5.2

RATTLING READERS 2

Finding Books

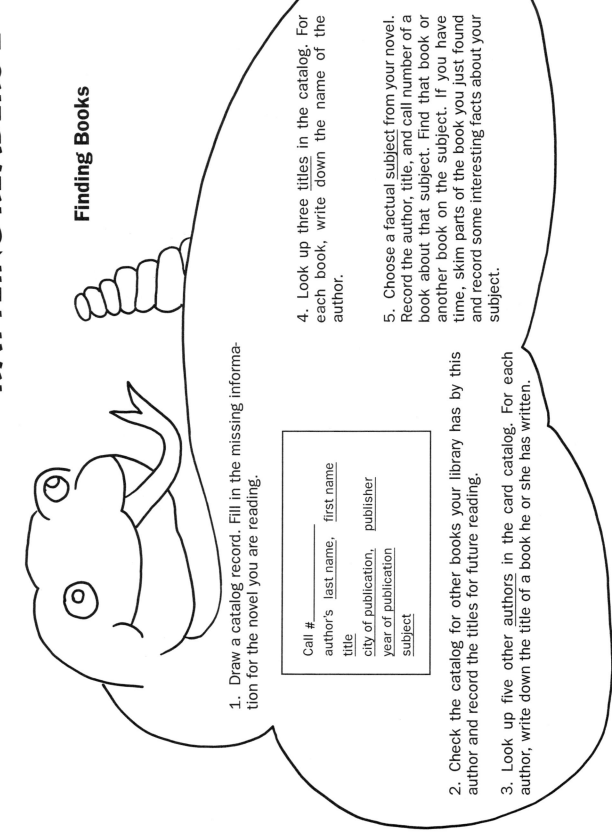

1. Draw a catalog record. Fill in the missing information for the novel you are reading.

   Call # _____
   author's last name, first name
   title
   city of publication, publisher
   year of publication
   subject

2. Check the catalog for other books your library has by this author and record the titles for future reading.

3. Look up five other authors in the card catalog. For each author, write down the title of a book he or she has written.

4. Look up three titles in the catalog. For each book, write down the name of the author.

5. Choose a factual subject from your novel. Record the author, title, and call number of a book about that subject. Find that book or another book on the subject. If you have time, skim parts of the book you just found and record some interesting facts about your subject.

56 From *Library Centers*. © 1997 Judith A. Sykes. Libraries Unlimited. (800) 237-6124.

Figure 5.3

RATTLING READERS 3

Author Research— Preparing a TV Interview

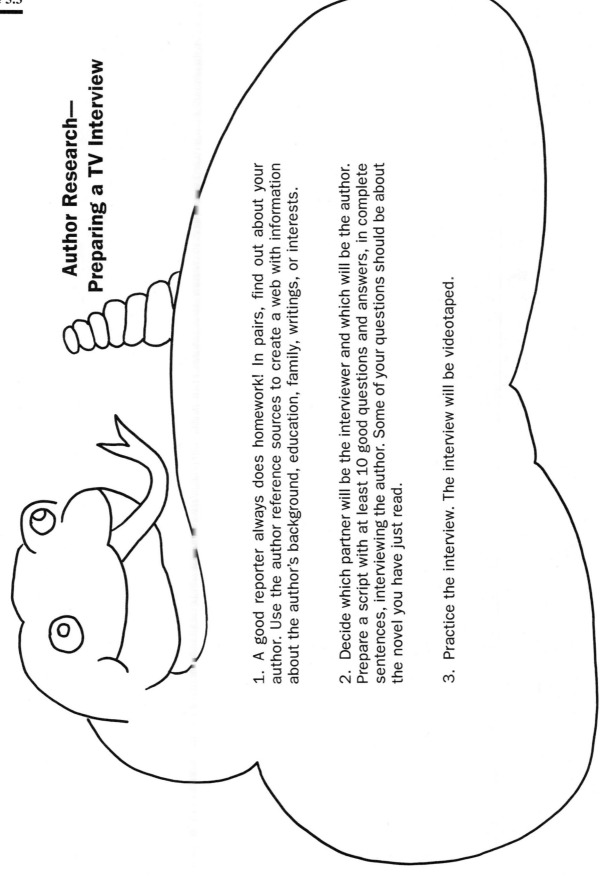

1. A good reporter always does homework! In pairs, find out about your author. Use the author reference sources to create a web with information about the author's background, education, family, writings, or interests.

2. Decide which partner will be the interviewer and which will be the author. Prepare a script with at least 10 good questions and answers, in complete sentences, interviewing the author. Some of your questions should be about the novel you have just read.

3. Practice the interview. The interview will be videotaped.

From *Library Centers* © 1997 Judith A. Sykes. Libraries Unlimited. (800) 237-6124.

Taping an interview

Watching a taped interview

RATTLING READERS 4

Materials Needed

- Rattling Readers 4 direction cards. (See fig. 5.4, p. 60.)
- Shoeboxes or other small boxes.
- Scissors, glue.
- Scraps of material, construction paper, yarn, and other construction materials.
- Art paper.
- Felt-tip markers, crayons, or paints.

Method

Students need to demonstrate comprehension of the concept of setting. Encourage them to focus on setting detail: background, objects, and design.

RATTLING READERS 5

Materials Needed

- Rattling Readers 5 direction cards. (See fig. 5.5, p. 61.)
- Art paper for portraits.

Method

This activity often needs a short lesson or talk during center time regarding the concept of fact in fiction. Some students will need assistance to extract character details from the prose. Writing will have to be edited. Students need to decide what information the author needed to research or be knowledgeable about to write their novels (for example, "mice" or "motorcycles" from Beverly Cleary's *The Mouse and the Motorcycle*).

Figure 5.4

RATTLING READERS 4

Setting

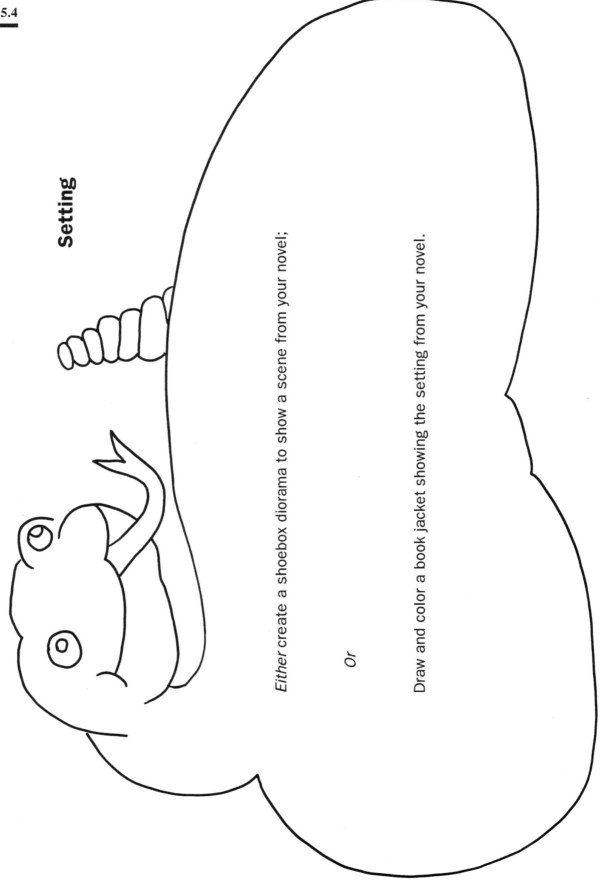

Either create a shoebox diorama to show a scene from your novel;

Or

Draw and color a book jacket showing the setting from your novel.

Figure 5.5

RATTLING READERS 5

Characterization

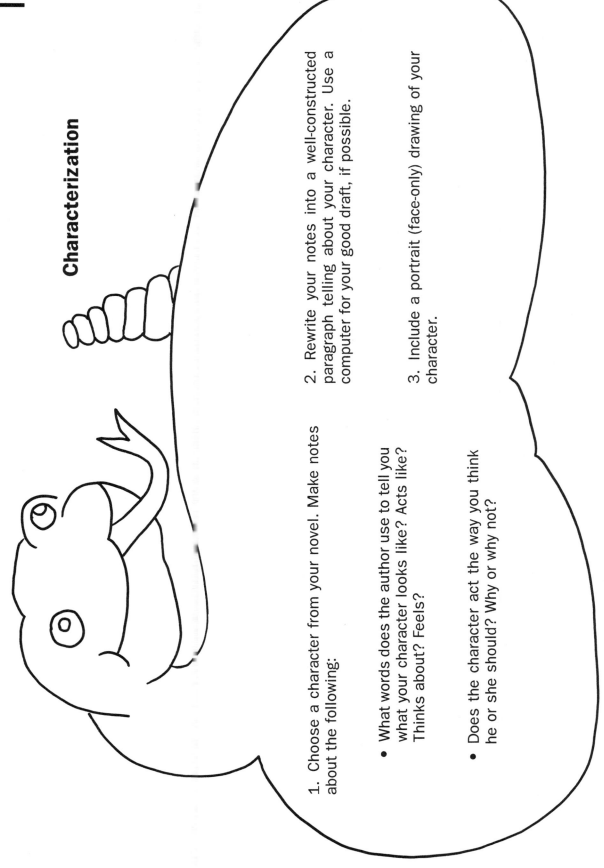

1. Choose a character from your novel. Make notes about the following:

- What words does the author use to tell you what your character looks like? Acts like? Thinks about? Feels?

- Does the character act the way you think he or she should? Why or why not?

2. Rewrite your notes into a well-constructed paragraph telling about your character. Use a computer for your good draft, if possible.

3. Include a portrait (face-only) drawing of your character.

From *Library Centers* © 1997 Judith A. Sykes. Libraries Unlimited. (800) 237-6124.

Figure 5.6

RATTLING READERS
Checklist

Student Name: _____

Novel Read: _____

Author: _____

CENTER	STUDENT COMMENTS	TEACHER COMMENTS
1. Author Bibliography		
__ 5 authors, 2 titles		
2. Finding Books		
__ Catalog record, list		
__ Catalog searches		
3. Author Research		
__ Web		
__ Interview script		
__ Video		
4. Setting		
__ Diorama *or*		
__ Book jacket		
5. Characterization		
__ Paragraph		
__ Portrait		

From *Library Centers*. © 1997 Judith A. Sykes. Libraries Unlimited. (800) 237-6124.

BOOK BASICS

Chapter Six

This next level of library centers is also facilitated by use of a reader's workshop approach. Having students read books that they themselves chose and pick their own authors to research gives authentic focus to the skills and activities. At least one to five other students will also have chosen the same novel, so there will be good opportunities for group discussion and project sharing. The centers can introduce the reader's workshop as part of a broad program to build a community of readers, involving the librarian, or they can enhance such a program based in the classroom. Often the centers demonstrate some of the literary and presentation skills students need to develop as they continue to read more novels.

Teachers can choose a variety of ways to implement these library centers. The teacher-librarian can begin the process with a booktalk; he or she may also become a participant in reading student response journals as time permits. Centers generally involve two hours of library time, though some students will need extra time to finish or extend projects. Teachers might reserve 12 days in the library (six weeks, two days each week), giving students classroom days in between to finish centers; other schedules may work better depending on how the library is scheduled. Students should be able to work with increasing independence at this level, but teachers will have to circulate to centers where assistance or task monitoring is necessary.

The evaluation checklist shown at the end of this chapter in figure 6.9, on page 75, may be used as an adjunct to student report cards or as another way to inform parents about the student's progress on an interim basis.

BOOK BASICS 1

Materials Needed

- Book Basics 1 direction cards. (See fig. 6.1, p. 65.)
- Examples of letter formats. (See figs. 6.2a and 6.2b, p. 66.)
- Author reference sources, such as *Something About the Author, Junior Authors,* "Junior Discovering Authors" CD-ROM, Internet sites.
- Writing paper and envelopes.

Method

Students may need assistance at this center with the author reference books; a general introduction could be done before you start the center. Check with students occasionally, as they may find the reading levels of some of the sources difficult. Letters to the authors should be edited and mailed. Some authors may accept e-mail from students, and this would be a good opportunity to teach students how to send an e-mail using the Internet.

Learning about authors

Figure 6.1

1 Author Research and Letter

1. Use the author reference sources in the library to research the author of your novel. Draw an "author web" in your notes— put the name of the author in the center and draw four circles or boxes around it with these headings:

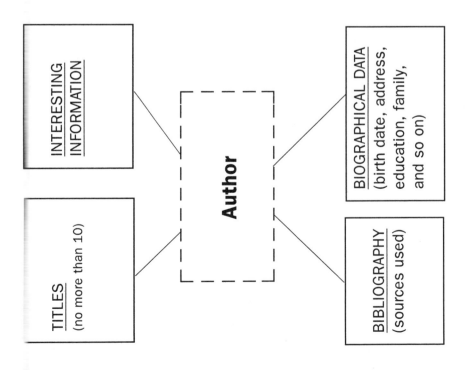

2. Now that you have finished researching the author of your novel, compose a letter to him or her. Use a word processor if available. If your author is no longer living, you may wish to write to the publisher of his or her books or to write to another of your favorite living authors. Use correct format (see examples). Address the envelope. Mail it to the author.

Address format example:

Ms. R. Jenkins
351 Milrise St.
Houston, TX 00000

Figure 6.2a

- *Letter format example:*

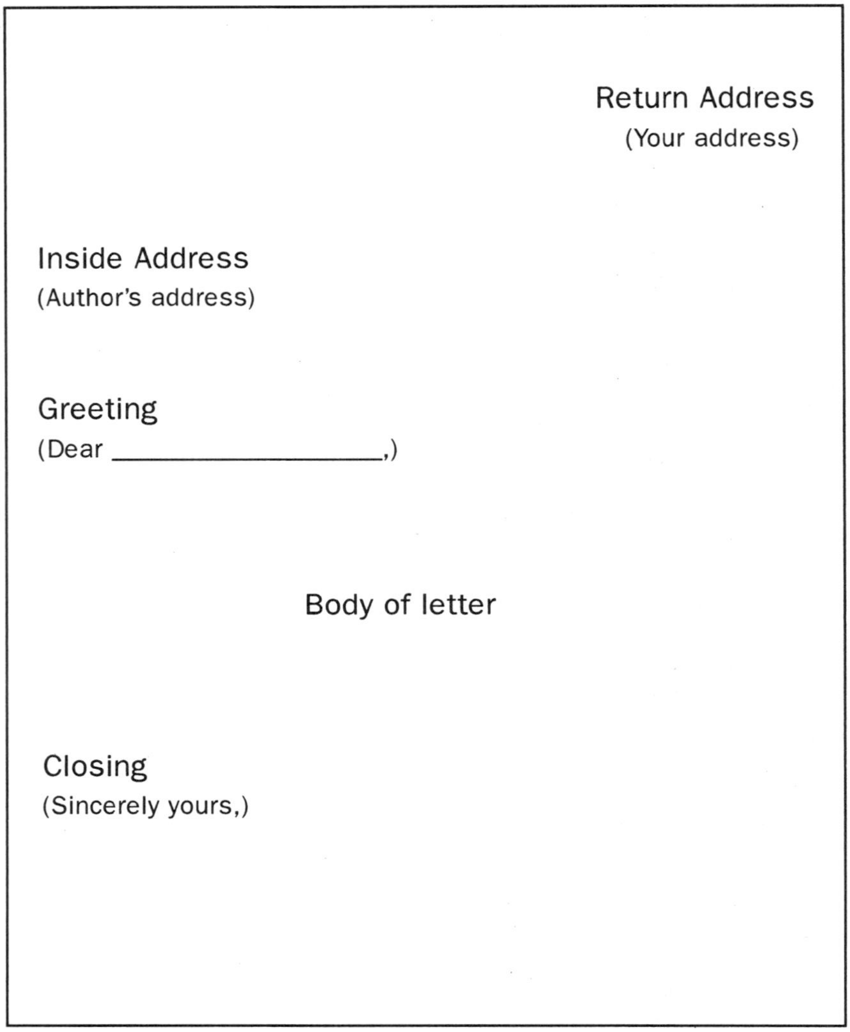

Return Address
(Your address)

Inside Address
(Author's address)

Greeting
(Dear _____,)

Body of letter

Closing
(Sincerely yours,)

Figure 6.2b

- *Envelope format example:*

Return Address
(Your address)

STAMP

Author's Address

From *Library Centers*. © 1997 Judith A. Sykes. Libraries Unlimited. (800) 237-6124.

BOOK BASICS 2

Materials Needed

- Book Basics 2 direction cards. (See fig. 6.3, p. 68.)
- Video camera and videotapes. If your school does not own a video camera, consider renting or borrowing one; if that is not an option, these presentations could be done on audiotape or live.

Method

Teachers can prepare their students by discussing the concept of character. Student scripts will have to be edited. A quiet area of the library should be set aside for videotaping. Students will also need a lesson on using the video camera, as each student should have a chance to film and be filmed. Groups may need assistance with directing the interviews and may need ideas for creating simple costumes and props.

BOOK BASICS 3

Materials Needed

- Book Basics 3 direction cards. (See fig. 6.4, p. 69.)
- Example of correct bibliographic form. (See fig. 6.5, p. 70.)
- Forty to fifty strips with names of authors at sixth-grade reading level, based on your collection.

Method

Students may need reminders about or assistance working with the catalog, whether card or electronic. If the books corresponding to their chosen author strips are out in circulation, they can use the catalog to complete the work. Some students will need encouragement and assistance at the bookshelves locating the actual materials. Bibliographies will have to be edited.

Figure 6.3

2 Character Videotape

Use correct script format, as shown in the sample, to write a script interviewing your favorite character from your novel. Use a word processor if available. Videotape the interview. Use costumes or simple props to add interest.

Sample Script Format:

"Gollum" from THE HOBBIT by J. R. R. Tolkien
(character)   (title)   (author)

Interviewer:
Today we will meet one of the trickiest characters from The Hobbit.

Gollum:
Precious is not tricky! Precious was tricked by a nasty hobbit!

Interviewer:
And who was this hobbit? Tell us about the trick.

(Continue with your own questions as appropriate for the novel and character you have chosen.)

Figure 6.4

3 Catalog Records—Locating Fiction

1. Draw a catalog record of your novel. Follow this sample.

Call #: _____

Author: _____

Title: _____

Publisher: _____

Date: _____

Subject: _____

2. Use the catalog to make a list of other books by the author of your novel.

3. Choose five author strips from the center. Go to the junior bookshelves and find two books by each author. Use the strips to mark the place on the shelf as you record the author, title, publisher, and copyright date of each book.

4. Record this information in correct bibliographic form. (See sample.) Use a word processor if available. You should now have a list of 10 new books to enjoy reading!

From *Library Center*. © 1997 Judith A. Sykes. Libraries Unlimited. (800) 237-6124.

Figure 6.5

- *Correct Bibliographic Form*
   *Look closely at the correct punctuation— check your work!

FICTION BIBLIOGRAPHY

Author's name (last name first, correct alphabetical order)	Titles (underlined)	Publisher	Year
Blume, Judy.	Fudge-a-mania. Dell, 1990.		
	Superfudge. Scholastic, 1980.		
Lunn, Janet.	Root Cellar. Methuen, 1979.		
	Twelve Dancing Princesses. Methuen, 1979.		

BOOK BASICS 4

Materials Needed

- Book Basics 4 direction cards. (See fig. 6.6, p. 71.)
- Encyclopedias/CD-ROM.
- Internet if available.

Method

Students will need assistance with choosing a factual topic from a novel and locating topics from reference materials, as well as in reading through the reference materials and making notes. This is a good time to introduce tips on using key words and phrases. Their work will require editing.

This center can be used to introduce the "notepad" feature of many CD-ROMs, such as Microsoft "Encarta." This feature allows students to "cut and paste" sections from their topic onto a word processor, where they can then rewrite their notes into their own words. They can also cut and paste graphics into their short reports. Internet and Web sites can also be used this way.

From *Library Centers.* © 1997 Judith A. Sykes. Libraries Unlimited. (800) 237-6124.

Figure 6.6

4 Novel Research

Choose a factual subject from your book. Research this subject, using at least two sources, and write a short report about it. Use a word processor if available.

Include a diagram(s) such as a drawing or sketch of your own, a map, a graph, computer art, or a printout from a CD-ROM or Web site.

From *Library Center*. © 1997 Judith A. Sykes. Libraries Unlimited. (800) 237-6124.

BOOK BASICS 5

Materials Needed

- Book Basics 5 direction cards. (See fig. 6.7, p. 73.)
- Enough bookmarks with the Dewey classifications on them so that each student can have one.

Method

Students may need assistance locating the Dewey sections in your library. Usually if you take them to the 000s and help them select an interesting book, they will continue independently through the rest of the library. They will need editing assistance with their bibliographies.

Finding books

BOOK BASICS 6

Materials Needed

- Book Basics 6 direction cards. (See fig. 6.8, p. 74.)
- Poster paper, scissors, glue, colored pencils.

Method

Teachers need to discuss with students the components of plot: problem, rising action, climax, resolution. Students will need assistance finding these events in their novels and editing their work.

Figure 6.7

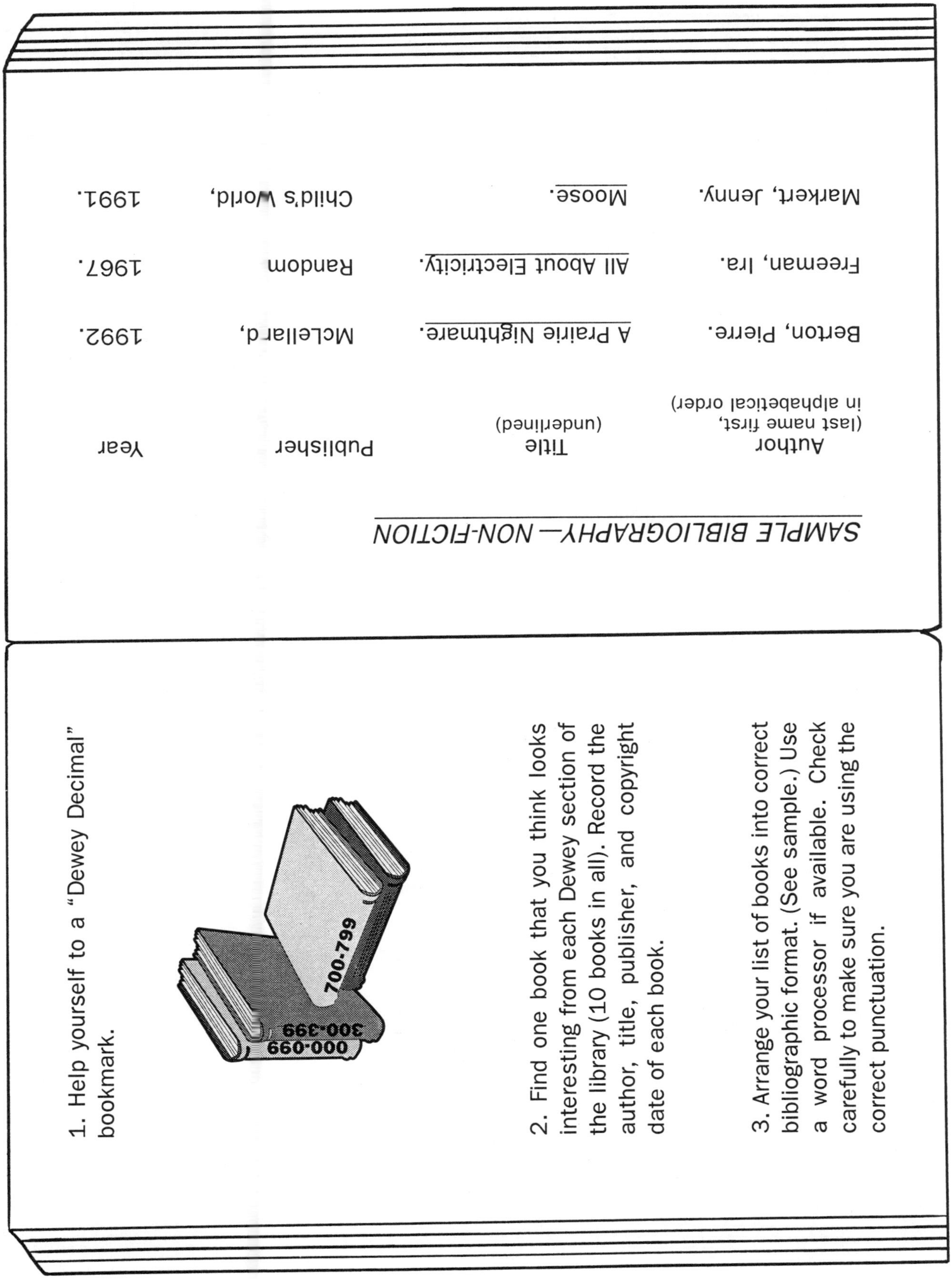

5 Locating Non-Fiction

1. Help yourself to a "Dewey Decimal" bookmark.

2. Find one book that you think looks interesting from each Dewey section of the library (10 books in all). Record the author, title, publisher, and copyright date of each book.

3. Arrange your list of books into correct bibliographic format. (See sample.) Use a word processor if available. Check carefully to make sure you are using the correct punctuation.

SAMPLE BIBLIOGRAPHY—NON-FICTION

Author (last name first, in alphabetical order)	Title (underlined)	Publisher	Year
Berton, Pierre.	A Prairie Nightmare.	McLelland,	1992.
Freeman, Ira.	All About Electricity.	Random	1957.
Markert, Jenny.	Moose.	Child's World,	1991.

From *Library Centers*. © 1997 Judith A. Sykes. Libraries Unlimited. (800) 237-6124.

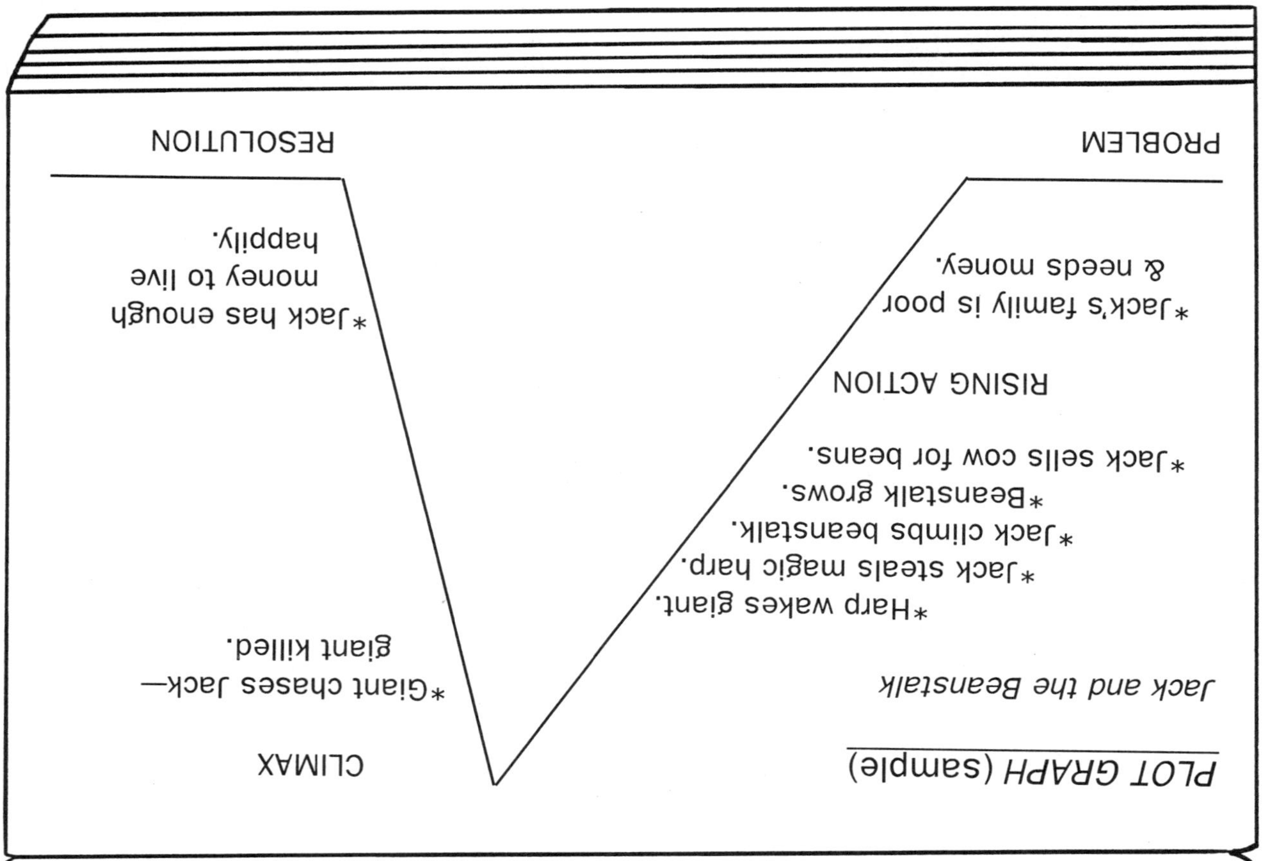

6 Plot

Design a "plot graph" of your project novel showing the events of the story. (See sample.) Have your story events edited. Do your good copy on a word processor if available, experimenting with fonts for labels and titles. Draw at least three illustrations to go with your points. Glue the words and illustrations onto a poster in the form of a graph.

PLOT GRAPH (sample)

Jack and the Beanstalk

CLIMAX

*Giant chases Jack—
giant killed.

*Harp wakes giant.
*Jack steals magic harp.
*Jack climbs beanstalk.
*Beanstalk grows.
*Jack sells cow for beans.

RISING ACTION

*Jack's family is poor
& needs money.

*Jack has enough
money to live
happily.

PROBLEM

RESOLUTION

Figure 6.8

Figure 6.9

BOOK BASICS
Checklist

Student Name: _____

Novel Title: _____

Author: _____

CENTER	STUDENT COMMENTS	TEACHER COMMENTS
1. Author Research and Letter		
__ Web		
__ Letter written		
__ Letter sent		
2. Character Videotape		
__ Script		
__ Videotaping		
3. Catalog Records—Locating Fiction		
__ Fiction		
__ Bibliography		
4. Novel Research		
__ Short report		
5. Locating Non-Fiction		
__ Bibliography		
6. Plot		
__ Words		
__ Illustrations		
__ Poster		

From *Library Centers*. © 1997 Judith A. Sykes. Libraries Unlimited. (800) 237-6124.

VICTORIAN HOLIDAY TRADITIONS

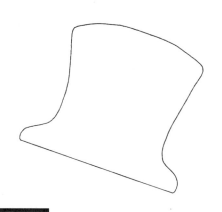

Chapter Seven

These centers are based on Charles Dickens's *A Christmas Carol*. Due to the challenging language of the novel, these centers are best used with upper elementary students. Teachers can present the book to classes as a novel study. Students from all cultures enjoy this timeless novel in the context of classic literature and historical study, although other novels could easily be adapted to the centers' activities. Often local professional theater companies produce "A Christmas Carol," and students might enjoy a field trip to see such a presentation. Many excellent videos are also available, including the classic Alastair Sim film version.

Classes might begin to work on these centers in mid-November, in preparation for a seasonal family night of viewing work and watching presentations of scenes from the novel. Classes could make Victorian Christmas cards to invite parents and other guests to the event, and might prepare plum pudding and steaming mugs of wassail for visitors to sample.

The evaluation checklist at the end of this chapter (fig. 7.8, p. 88) can be used for an interim student report or sent home with the report card.

VICTORIAN HOLIDAY TRADITIONS 1

Materials Needed

- Victorian Holiday Traditions 1 direction cards. (See fig. 7.1, p. 79.)
- Books or photos from your library or other sources depicting wealthy and poor families in Victorian England.
- Art paper and supplies for the newspaper format or access to word processors that will produce columns, tables, and so on.

Method

Students will need assistance with editing and possibly organizing the comparative aspects of this writing.

VICTORIAN HOLIDAY TRADITIONS 2

Materials Needed

- Victorian Holiday Traditions 2 direction cards. (See fig. 7.2, p. 80.)
- Author reference sources about Charles Dickens. Ones with photographs, such as *Something About the Author* or the Gale CD-ROM called "Junior Authors," are preferable.
- "Cue" cards, such as 3" x 5" recipe cards.
- Blank audio- or videotapes.

Method

Students will need assistance composing and editing their speeches. They will also need tips and helpful critiques when rehearsing their speeches. If classes are unfamiliar with taping procedures, a lesson in the library on using the video camera or tape recorders may be in order.

Figure 7.1

VICTORIAN HOLIDAY TRADITIONS

1

Living Conditions of Victorian Children

Look at the pictures and photos. Discuss them with your group.

Pretend you are a reporter from your local newspaper who fell asleep at your desk and discovered upon awakening that Marley's Ghost had taken you back in time to Victorian England. Write a newspaper report on the differences in the lifestyles of wealthy and poor children in Victorian times. Remember the five "Ws" of reporting: who, what, when, where, and why. Design your good copy as a newspaper layout.

From *Library Centers*. © 1997 Judith A. Sykes. Libraries Unlimited. (800) 237-6124.

Figure 7.2

From *Library Centers*. © 1997 Judith A. Sykes. Libraries Unlimited. (800) 237-6124.

VICTORIAN HOLIDAY TRADITIONS 3

Materials Needed

- Victorian Holiday Traditions 3 direction cards. (See fig. 7.3, p. 82.)
- Question cards. (See fig. 7.4, p. 83.)
- Extra copies of the magazine article.
- Construction paper, scissors, glue, coloring materials.
- Samples of pop-up books.

Method

As in some of the other centers, *National Geographic* magazine is used as a source for students to develop skill in studying pictures and reading picture captions for information. Some students find the articles to be at too advanced a reading level, but the ready availability of this magazine makes it an invaluable source. This magazine is usually available in schools, and extra copies, especially of older issues (April 1974, in this case), can be gleaned from garage sales, parent collections, or the National Geographic Society itself. Once students discover what an interesting source it is, circulation of issues of this periodical really goes up! You may also find the necessary information for the center in another reference or electronic source, though.

Students may need ideas in getting started with pop-up books. Share examples of these types of books and demonstrate ideas for making them. If word processors are available, the sentences for the pop-up books could be produced on them. This assignment could also work as a hypermedia presentation if your school has multimedia software such as "HyperStudio" (Windows) or "HyperCard" (Macintosh).

VICTORIAN HOLIDAY TRADITIONS 4

Materials Needed

- Victorian Holiday Traditions 4 direction cards. (See fig. 7.5, p. 84.)
- Encyclopedias, CD-ROMs.
- Christmas shapes to trace: Dickens-style hat, Santa, bells, trees, present, and so on.

Method

Students will need some assistance locating information and identifying key words. Paragraphs will require editing. If word processors are available, students should be encouraged to write their paragraphs on the computer.

Figure 7.3

82 From *Library Centers*. © 1997 Judith A. Sykes. Libraries Unlimited. (800) 237-6124.

Figure 7.4

QUESTION CARDS

Use in conjunction with "The England of Charles Dickens," *National Geographic* magazine, April 1974.

---

1. The Life of Charles Dickens

p. 444   How old is Dickens in this picture? Why was Dickens's father imprisoned in 1824? When Dickens's father was sent to prison, Charles was sent to work in a London factory. What was his job?

p. 451   What was the name of the "depressing institution" in which Dickens worked? How long did he work there? What did he do next?

Dickens never forgave the law profession for "the cruel penal code and appalling working conditions." Give an example of the working conditions that his novels helped to reform.

---

2. The Novels of Charles Dickens

p. 452   Dickens wrote 15 novels. Record the names and dates of five of them, especially ones that you have heard of before.

---

3. Famous Characters

p. 459   Many of Dickens's characters were inspired by people he knew, such as his first wife's younger sister Mary. Which character did Mary influence?

p. 474   Another of Dickens's famous characters was born at Marshalsea Prison. Why was she born in prison?

p. 464   What is the name of Dickens's best-loved character?

From *Library Centers* © 1997 Judith A. Sykes. Libraries Unlimited. (800) 237-6124.

Figure 7.5

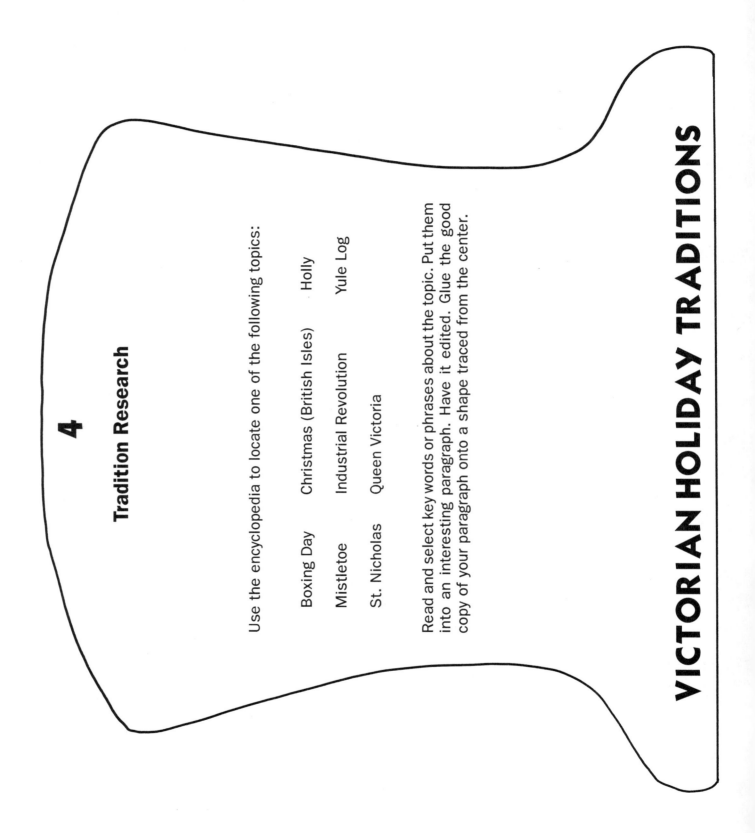

4

Tradition Research

Use the encyclopedia to locate one of the following topics:

Boxing Day   Christmas (British Isles)   Holly

Mistletoe   Industrial Revolution   Yule Log

St. Nicholas   Queen Victoria

Read and select key words or phrases about the topic. Put them into an interesting paragraph. Have it edited. Glue the good copy of your paragraph onto a shape traced from the center.

VICTORIAN HOLIDAY TRADITIONS

84 From *Library Centers*. © 1997 Judith A. Sykes. Libraries Unlimited. (800) 237-6124.

VICTORIAN HOLIDAY TRADITIONS 5

Materials Needed

- Victorian Holiday Traditions 5 direction cards. (See fig. 7.6, p. 86.)
- Dictionaries.
- Examples of word puzzles, such as crosswords or word searches.
- Electronic crossword or word-search programs, if available, such as "Crossword Magic" (Apple IIE) and "Expert Crosswords" (IBM).

Method

Students may need assistance in understanding the correct meanings for the words in the context of the story and making them into puzzle clues. Electronic puzzle programs are very motivating to students and let them think about applying definitions to puzzle clues.

VICTORIAN HOLIDAY TRADITIONS 6

Materials Needed

- Victorian Holiday Traditions 6 direction cards. (See fig. 7.7, p. 87.)
- Mural paper.
- Scissors, glue, paints, crayons, and other similar materials.

Method

Students should design their writing to resemble a memo. If they have access to word processors, most programs have a "columns" function for creating memos. This work should be edited for descriptive detail. An alternative to creating the mural-size ghosts is to use clay or plasticine to make the ghosts, or to use 8.5" x 11" sketch paper for black-and-white ghost sketches.

Figure 7.6

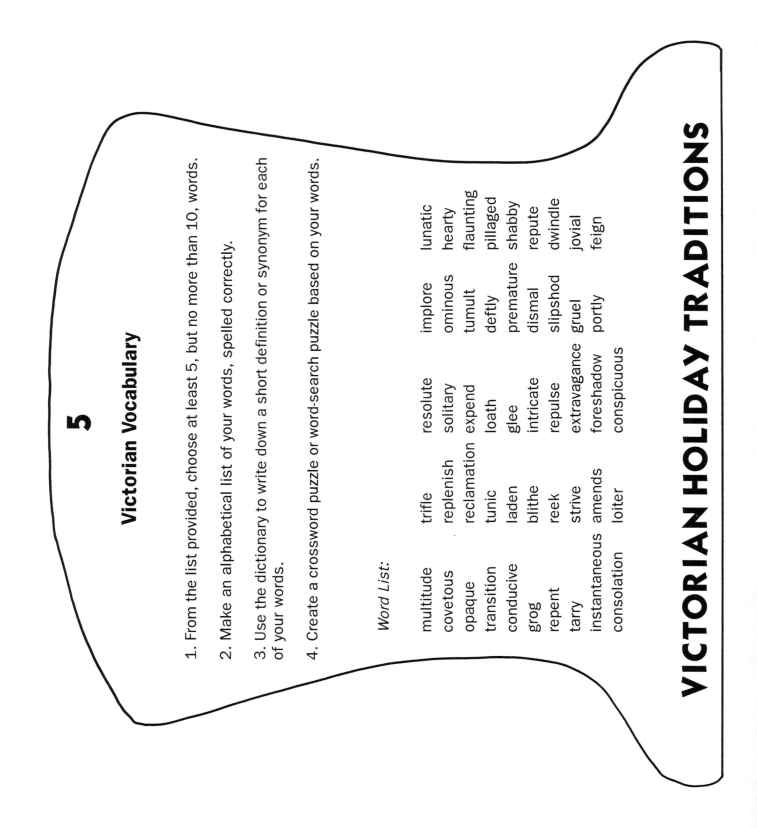

5

Victorian Vocabulary

1. From the list provided, choose at least 5, but no more than 10, words.
2. Make an alphabetical list of your words, spelled correctly.
3. Use the dictionary to write down a short definition or synonym for each of your words.
4. Create a crossword puzzle or word-search puzzle based on your words.

Word List:

multitude	trifle	resolute	implore	lunatic
covetous	replenish	solitary	ominous	hearty
opaque	reclamation	expend	tumult	flaunting
transition	tunic	loath	deftly	pillaged
conducive	laden	glee	premature	shabby
grog	blithe	intricate	dismal	repute
repent	reek	repulse	slipshod	dwindle
tarry	strive	extravagance	gruel	jovial
instantaneous	amends	foreshadow	portly	feign
consolation	loiter	conspicuous		

VICTORIAN HOLIDAY TRADITIONS

From *Library Centers.* © 1997 Judith A. Sykes. Libraries Unlimited. (800) 237-6124.

Figure 7.7

Figure 7.8

VICTORIAN HOLIDAY TRADITIONS
Checklist

Student Name: _____

CENTER	STUDENT COMMENTS	TEACHER COMMENTS
1. Living Conditions		
__ Newspaper report		
2. Author Research		
__ Speech		
__ Video		
3. *National Geographic*		
__ Answering questions		
__ Pop-up book		
4. Victorian Holiday Traditions		
__ Research paragraph		
__ Shape		
5. Vocabulary		
__ Definitions		
__ Crossword puzzle		
6. Ghosts of Christmas		
__ Memo		
__ Art project		

88   From *Library Centers*. © 1997 Judith A. Sykes. Libraries Unlimited. (800) 237-6124.

EGYPT OLD AND NEW

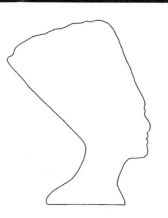

Chapter Eight

These centers, based on *The Egypt Game* by Zilpha Keatley Snyder, enhance a novel study and could be adapted to other novels. They also introduce an ancient civilization to upper elementary-level students. At least 14 library/media center sessions will be needed for the students to gather the information for the projects. Teachers can begin the centers at any point in the novel study. The students enjoy sharing their work at the end of the sessions with classmates or parents.

The evaluation checklist at the end of this chapter (fig. 8.8, p. 101) can be used for an interim student report or sent home with the report card.

EGYPT OLD AND NEW 1

Materials Needed

- Egypt Old and New 1 direction cards. (See fig. 8.1, p. 90.)
- Books, pictures, and other resources. You may want to gather these at the center to save the students searching time, depending on how independent they are in search processes.
- "Sketch pads" (can be scrap paper stapled together or white art paper).
- Pencils. Ordinary ones will do, but if you have access to art pencils you may wish to have students use them in this activity.
- Book, poster (bought or made), and/or encyclopedia article of the hieroglyph alphabet.

Method

Students may need assistance in locating materials and using an index. These skills can also be taught or reviewed in preview sessions. Students may need to be encouraged as to their drawings, especially if they lack confidence in their artwork. Remind them to label their drawings and note the sources.

Figure 8.1

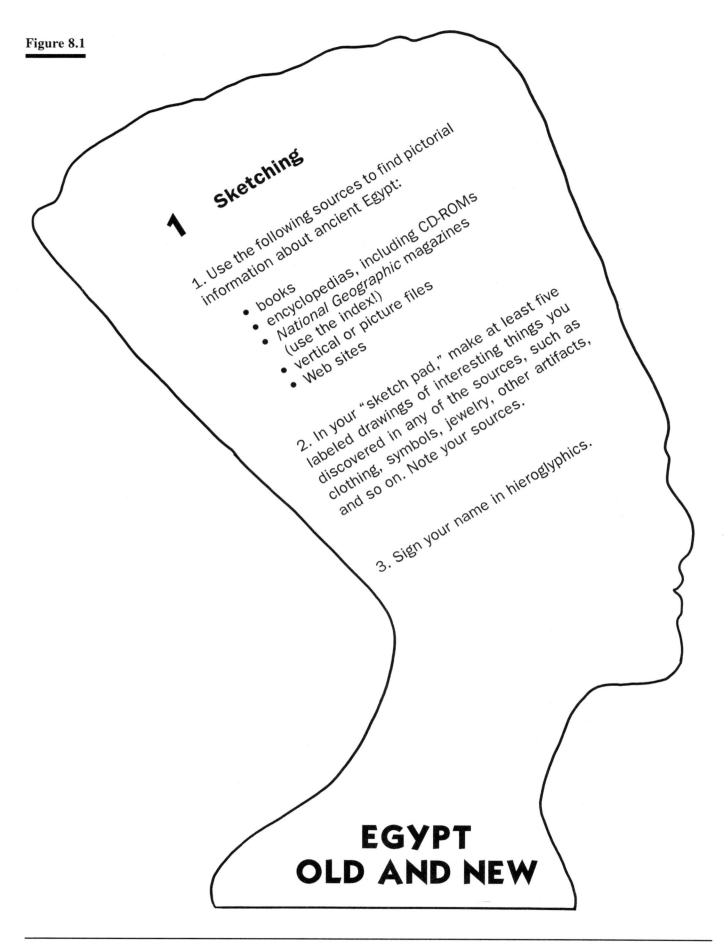

EGYPT OLD AND NEW 2

Materials Needed

- Egypt Old and New 2 direction cards. (See fig. 8.2, p. 92.)
- Access to encyclopedias or CD-ROMs.
- Art paper.
- Boxes, facial tissues, tape.

Method

Students may need assistance in locating appropriate and usable items for the third activity. They will also need advice or pictures to follow in designing their "tombs."

EGYPT OLD AND NEW 3

Materials Needed

- Egypt Old and New 3 direction cards. (See fig. 8.3, p. 93.)
- Extra copies of the novel.
- A box containing items that could be used as simple props or costumes, such as old scarves, jewelry, towels, sheets, hats, and so on.

Method

Teachers or the teacher-librarian will need to monitor and coach the process of group work. Some groups have difficulty deciding on a scene; some groups need help selecting parts and including all group members. If certain students don't want an acting part, perhaps they can narrate or mime. Coaching will be needed throughout rehearsals, and groups may need assistance with timing so that their scenes do not run too long or short.

91

Figure 8.2

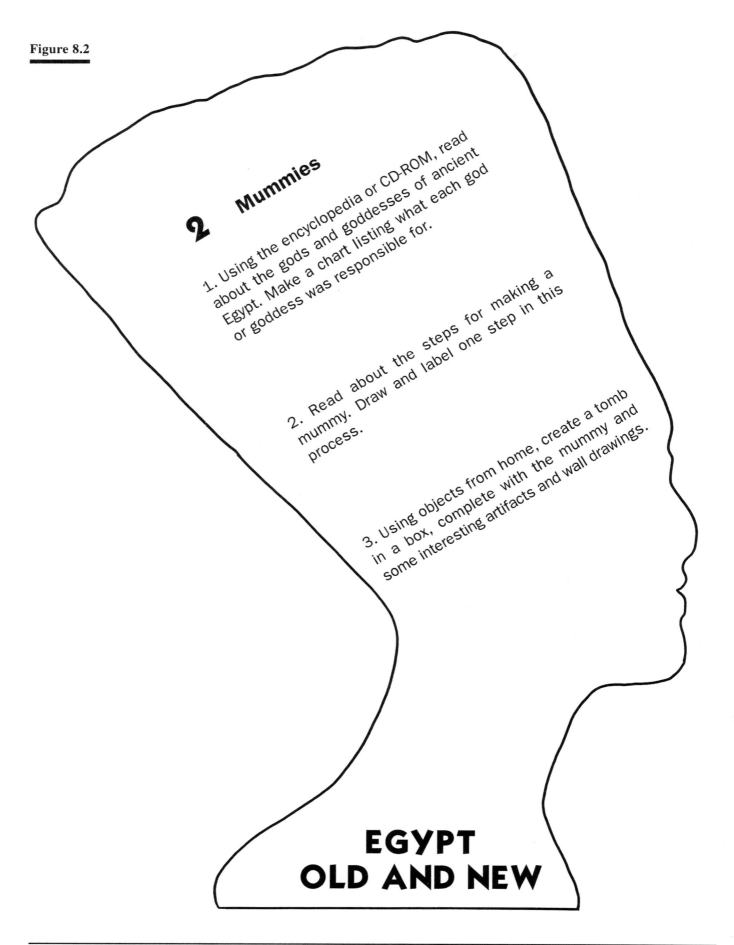

Figure 8.3

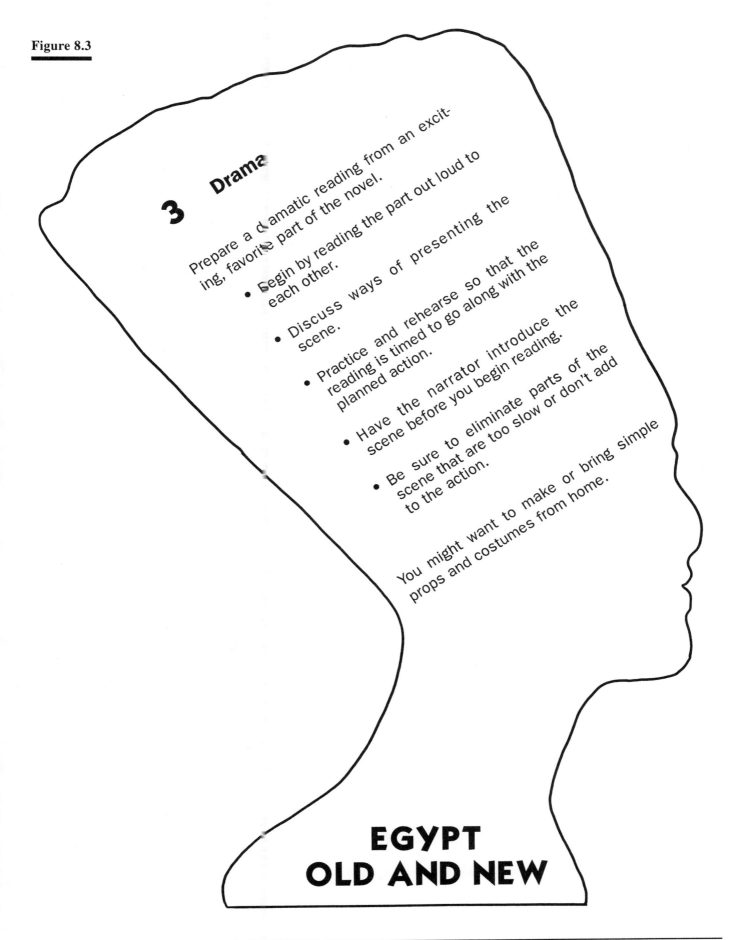

3 Drama

Prepare a dramatic reading from an exciting, favorite part of the novel.

- Begin by reading the part out loud to each other.
- Discuss ways of presenting the scene.
- Practice and rehearse so that the reading is timed to go along with the planned action.
- Have the narrator introduce the scene before you begin reading.
- Be sure to eliminate parts of the scene that are too slow or don't add to the action.

You might want to make or bring simple props and costumes from home.

EGYPT OLD AND NEW

From *Library Centers* © 1997 Judith A. Sykes. Libraries Unlimited. (800) 237-6124.

EGYPT OLD AND NEW 4

Materials Needed

- Egypt Old and New 4 direction cards. (See fig. 8.4, p. 95.)
- Pads of large chart paper.
- Thick colored felt-tip markers.
- Art paper.
- Copies of the novel.

Method

Groups may need assistance in beginning cooperative work on the chart. They may also need help in selecting character detail points from the novel. Poems will require editing; if possible, put them on a word processor.

EGYPT OLD AND NEW 5

Materials Needed

- Egypt Old and New 5 direction cards. (See fig. 8.5, p. 96.)
- Atlases or electronic atlases such as "PCGlobe," "Encarta," "PCMaps and Facts."
- White paper, 8.5" x 11" or larger.

Method

Before beginning these centers, discover how much map work students have done and how much preparation they might need before doing this type of work. Once at the center, students will need assistance in locating and placing some of the information, such as the elevations. They often forget to create a legend.

Figure 8.4

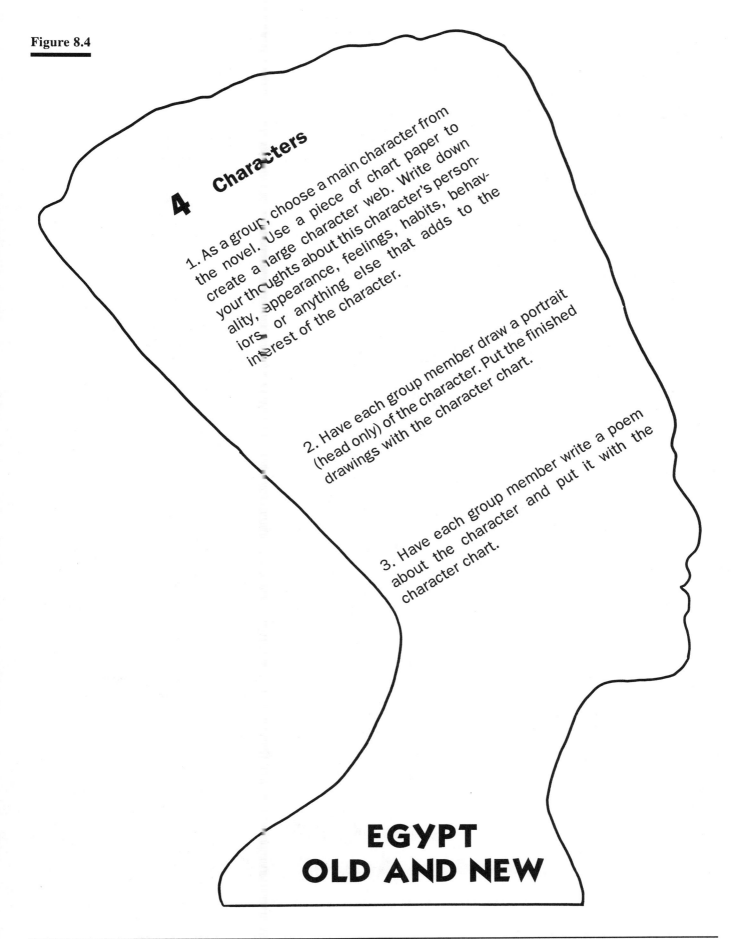

4 Characters

1. As a group, choose a main character from the novel. Use a piece of chart paper to create a large character web. Write down your thoughts about this character's personality, appearance, feelings, habits, behaviors, or anything else that adds to the interest of the character.

2. Have each group member draw a portrait (head only) of the character. Put the finished drawings with the character chart.

3. Have each group member write a poem about the character and put it with the character chart.

EGYPT OLD AND NEW

From *Library Centers*. © 1997 Judith A. Sykes. Libraries Unlimited. (800) 237-6124.

Figure 8.5

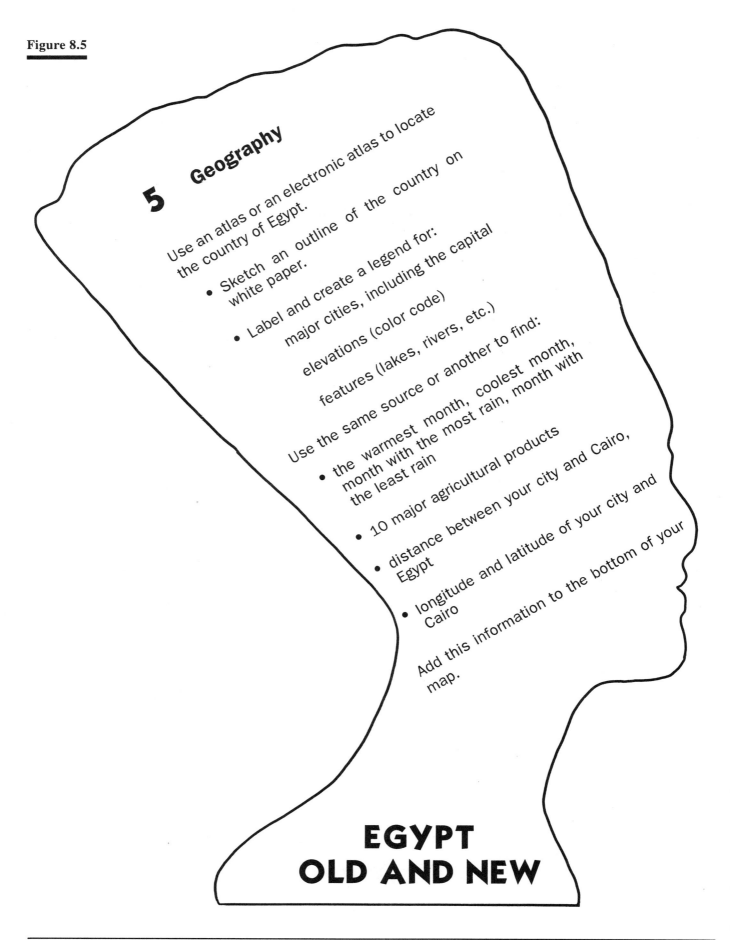

EGYPT OLD AND NEW 6

Materials Needed

- Egypt Old and New 5 direction cards. (See fig. 8.6, p. 98.)
- Author reference sources such as *Something About the Author.*
- Examples of correct letter format. (See fig. 6.2, p. 66.)
- Possibly stationery.

Method

Students may need a lesson or review on using author sources. They may also need help with reading for key facts from these sources. Discussion will occur about the content of the letter, particularly in the editing process. If the students have access to word processors, they may wish to write their letters on the computer or design their own stationery. Without word processors, they may still enjoy designing their own stationery and handwriting their letters. Teachers can collect the letters and mail them to the author in a single envelope.

Figure 8.6

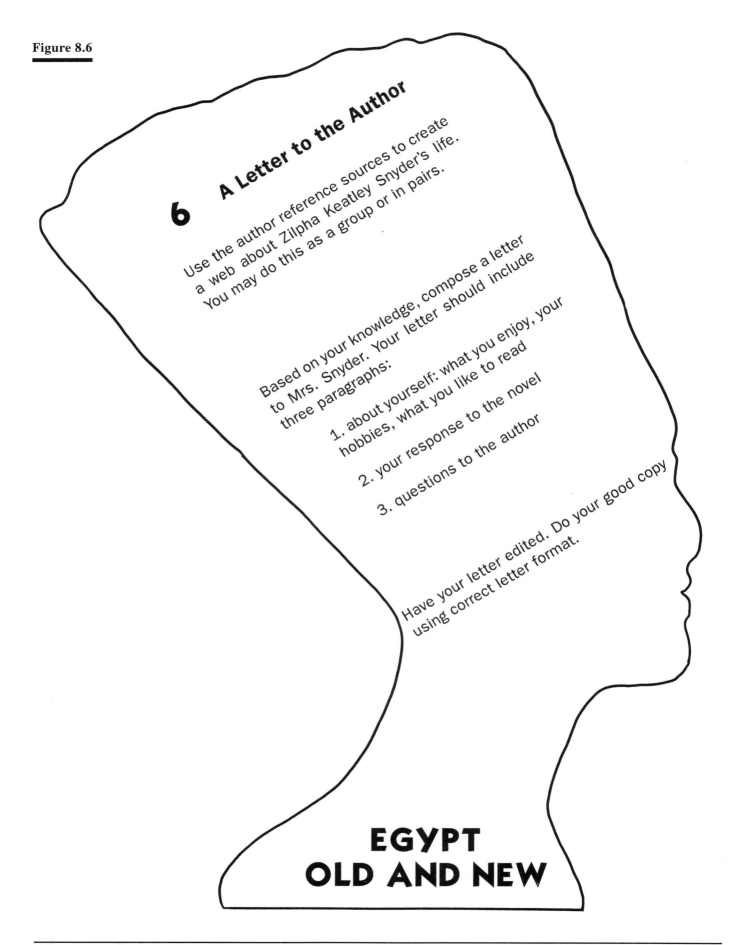

From *Library Centers*. © 1997 Judith A. Sykes. Libraries Unlimited. (800) 237-6124.

EGYPT OLD AND NEW 7

Materials Needed

- Egypt Old and New 7 direction cards. (See fig. 8.7, p. 100.)
- Reference sources, such as encyclopedias, CD-ROMs ("National Geographic Picture Atlas of the World" is a good one), and the Internet.
- Poster paper.

Method

Students may need assistance in locating information. They should be encouraged to present their rough work for editing, use a word processor where possible, and lay out their posters for balance prior to gluing.

Using a CD-ROM atlas

Figure 8.7

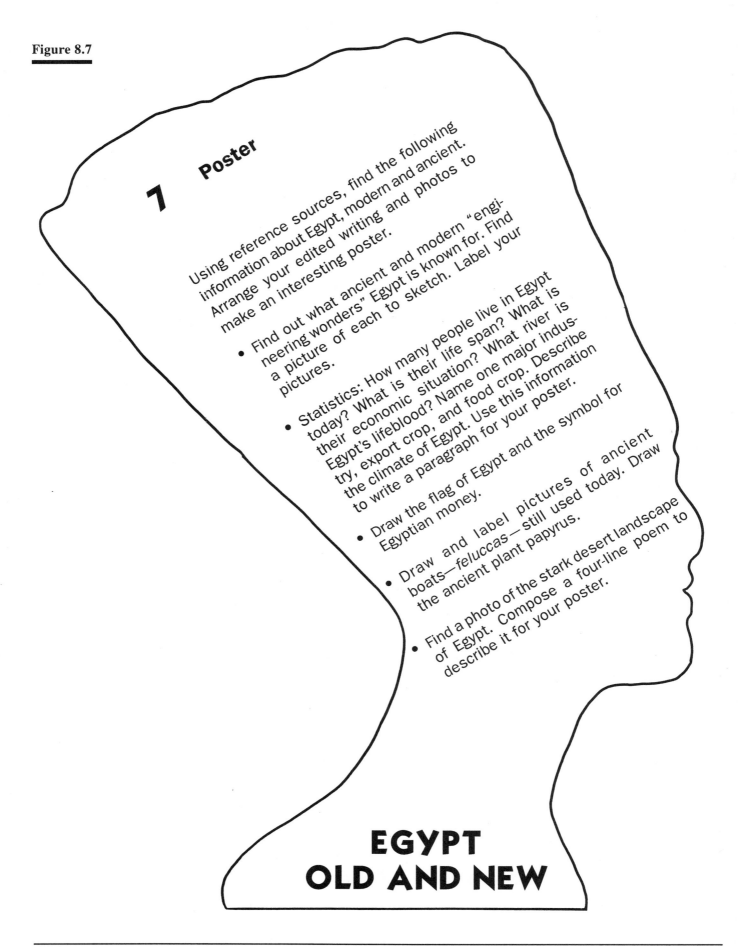

100 From *Library Centers*. © 1997 Judith A. Sykes. Libraries Unlimited. (800) 237-6124.

Figure 8.8

EGYPT OLD AND NEW
Checklist

Student Name and Hieroglyph: _____

CENTER	STUDENT COMMENTS	TEACHER COMMENTS
1. Sketches		
__ Five labeled sketches (signed in hieroglyphics)		
2. Mummies		
__ Chart		
__ Steps		
__ Diorama		
3. Drama		
__ Presentation of scene		
4. Character		
__ Group web		
__ Portrait		
__ Poem		
5. Geography		
__ Map with atlas		
__ Facts		
6. Author Research		
__ Web		
__ Letter		
7. Egypt Old and New		
__ Research		
__ Pictures, poem		
__ Poster		

From *Library Centers*. ∋ 1997 Judith A. Sykes. Libraries Unlimited. (800) 237-6124.

ANCIENT GREECE

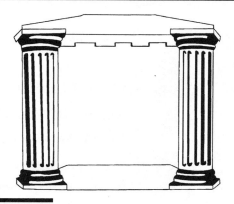

Chapter Nine

Study of an ancient civilization is a common curricular theme. This set of centers enhances an upper elementary-level study of ancient Greece with resource-based learning. These centers could easily be adapted and used in conjunction with the study of any other past civilization or culture. The centers take up to six weeks to complete, allowing about two hours of work per center per student. The centers often conclude with a celebration during which center work is displayed for other classes and/or parents. Some celebrations have also included a "lunchbox theater" for which parents and students prepared Greek dishes to share. For the theater portions, students perform scenes from Greek myths, give dramatic monologues, or narrate storyboards from the centers.

The evaluation checklist at the end of this chapter (fig. 9.7, p. 113) can be used for an interim student report or sent home with the report card.

ANCIENT GREECE 1

Materials Needed

- Ancient Greece 1 direction cards. (See fig. 9.1, p. 104.)
- A selection of books from your collection on ancient Greece. Check the indexes to make sure these books include diagrams of the Greek columns, information about the Acropolis, and information about moving stones; many books on ancient Greece include this information.
- Other reference sources, such as encyclopedias and CD-ROMs ("Encarta" is one CD-ROM that contains this information).
- 8.5" x 11" white drawing paper.

Method

Students may require assistance locating the information, as well as needing encouragement with their sketches. Diaries will have to be edited.

103

Figure 9.1

1

Architecture

Use the books and other reference sources at this center to research the following topics and complete the projects.

- Draw and label the three styles of architectural columns used in Greek buildings. Make each drawing about 10 inches. Do your good copy on white paper.

- Locate information about the Acropolis. Note the names of the buildings within the complex. Write a diary entry as if you were a young person who worked at the Acropolis every day. You live in the town of Athens and have to enter the gateway each morning. You are one of the many workers who must keep the Acropolis clean and tidy. Try to use as many of the names of the buildings as possible in your diary. Roll up and decorate your diary to resemble an ancient scroll.

- Locate diagrams or descriptions of two different methods the ancient Greeks used to move large stones for building. Draw and label these methods.

ANCIENT GREECE

104   From *Library Centers*. © 1997 Judith A. Sykes. Libraries Unlimited. (800) 237-6124.

Discussing information

Doing a CD-ROM search

105

ANCIENT GREECE 2

Materials Needed

- Ancient Greece 2 direction cards. (See fig. 9.2, p. 108.)
- Books, vertical file material, and other resources pertaining to the topics of Greek food and clothing. You may find good sources in other sections of your collection, such as costumes, clothing, and recipe books.
- Poster paper, art paper.

Method

Students may need help with poster or magazine layout and design. They may wish to use a word processor to assist with this, if one is available.

ANCIENT GREECE 3

Materials Needed

- Ancient Greece 3 direction cards. (See fig. 9.3, p. 109.)
- Books of myths, including picture books. Also use filmstrips or videos of popular Greek myths if you have them in your collection or available to borrow.
- Poster paper.

Method

Students may need coaching to complete this project as a group. They will need to share the initial decision and read together and then delegate specific tasks to group members. Some students may prefer to write or word process the sentences; another may wish to do some of the drawings; and so on. Each group member must be made to feel that he or she is contributing to the success of the whole project. Students will need assistance with the oral rehearsals of the storyboard.

ANCIENT GREECE 4

Materials Needed

- Ancient Greece 4 direction cards. (See fig. 9.4, p. 110.)
- Encyclopedias/CD-ROMs.
- Costume materials, such as sheets, toy swords, and other items from which to make props.

Method

Students may need assistance with summarizing the myth into a paragraph-length monologue. They need to know what a monologue is and that this particular oral assignment is individual. They will need to have their work edited and probably will also need rehearsal tips.

ANCIENT GREECE 5

Materials Needed

- Ancient Greece 5 direction cards. (See fig. 9.5, p. 111.)
- Books on ancient Greece; they often include chapters on science.
- Encyclopedias, CD-ROMs, information on the location of Web sites.
- Half-size poster paper.

Method

Students may need assistance with understanding some of the inventions they come across in the research, for example, the catapult or the Hippocratic oath. Their work will require editing, and they may need suggestions for poster or model design.

ANCIENT GREECE 6

Materials Needed

- Ancient Greece 6 direction cards. (See fig. 9.6, p. 112.)
- Books on ancient Greece; check indexes for information about shipping.
- Encyclopedias, CD-ROMs (such as "Encarta," or "Ancient Lands").
- Half-size poster paper.
- Maps of the Mediterranean.

Method

Students may need assistance in finding information and in understanding certain topics, such as trade routes Often students draw their Mediterranean maps freehand, but you can include copies of maps at the center if you choose. Students' work will need editing.

107

Figure 9.2

2
Food and Clothing

At this center, choose either project A or project B. You may work with a partner.

A. FOOD: Read about a modern-day Greek family and the food they prepare and eat. Many of these foods could have been served in ancient Greece.

Make a poster, drawing the dishes as they would be cooked and served. Try to include authentic serving dishes. Label each item as to what it is and what ingredients are in it. Try to keep colors accurate. You may want to give your poster a three-dimensional look by gluing on items such as rice, models made of plasticine, and so on.

If you wish, you may prepare a dish for the class to sample!

B. CLOTHING: Using books, encyclopedias, or whatever sources you wish, make a series of labeled drawings about the clothing worn by different people in Greek society. This could be presented in booklet form as a "fashion magazine" from ancient Greece or as a fashion show (old sheets are invaluable).

ANCIENT GREECE

From *Library Centers.* © 1997 Judith A. Sykes. Libraries Unlimited. (800) 237-6124.

Figure 9.3

3
Mythology Storyboard

This is a group project!

1. Using the materials provided, decide as a group which Greek myth you will use for your storyboard.

2. Review the myth carefully together. It is important that you understand the events. Read or view another version of your story if available in the materials provided.

3. Create a storyboard of the myth by:

- listing 12 main events from the story
- writing an informative and detailed sentence for each event
- gluing the sentences on poster paper in order
- illustrating each sentence
- putting each group member's name on the poster
- presenting the storyboard to the class

ANCIENT GREECE

From *Library Centers* © 1997 Judith A. Sykes. Libraries Unlimited. (800) 237-6124.

Figure 9.4

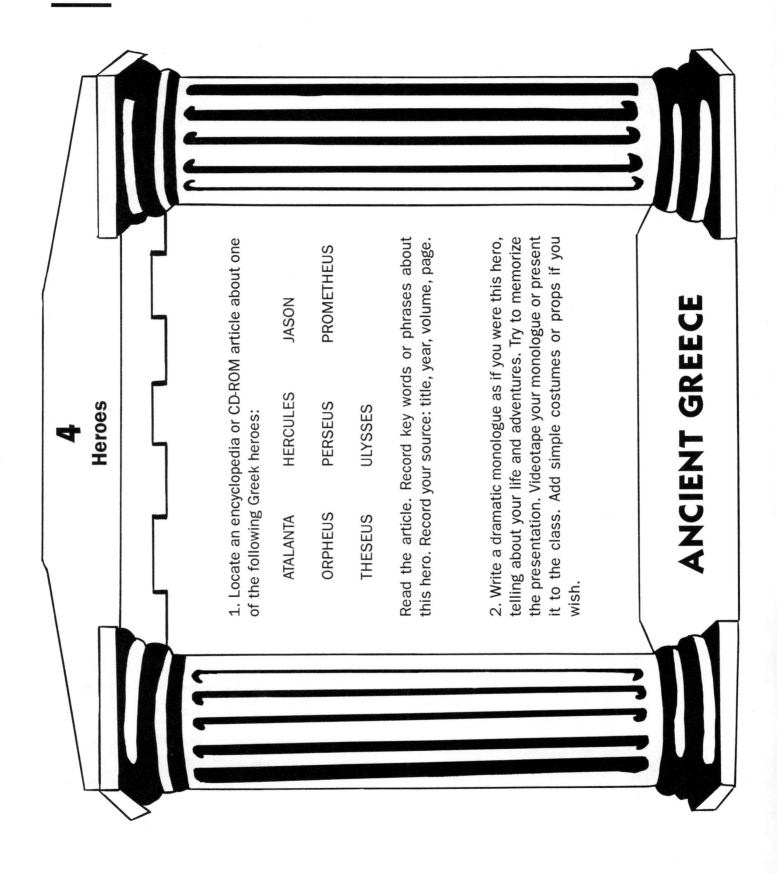

110   From *Library Centers*. © 1997 Judith A. Sykes. Libraries Unlimited. (800) 237-6124.

Figure 9.5

From *Library Centers*. © 1997 Judith A. Sykes. Libraries Unlimited. (800) 237-6124.

Figure 9.6

6
Transportation

Using library books or other sources, read and take notes about the two main reasons ships were so important to the ancient Greeks:

- trade (cargo ships) and
- military (war ships).

Choose **one** of the following activities:

1. Do a small poster report (with illustrations and written information) on the Greek warship, the *trireme*. Tell about its design and how it was used in battle.

2. Complete a map of the Mediterranean Sea, showing the area and colonies where Greek merchant ships carried goods for trade. Label at least five main trading centers. Make a list of the cargo carried.

3. Make a concept poster to show the different hazards and risks that sailing presented for the ancient Greeks. Hints: navigation, storms, pirates, unseasoned timber.

ANCIENT GREECE

From *Library Centers*. © 1997 Judith A. Sykes. Libraries Unlimited. (800) 237-6124.

Figure 9.7

ANCIENT GREECE
Checklist

Student Name: _____

CENTER	STUDENT COMMENTS	TEACHER COMMENTS
1. Architecture		
__ Columns		
__ Diary		
__ Moving stones		
2. Food/Clothing		
__ Poster *or*		
__ Fashion magazine		
3. Storyboards		
__ Board		
__ Presentations		
4. Heroes		
__ Monologue written		
__ Monologue presented		
5. Science		
__ List		
__ Poster *or* model		
__ Script		
6. Transportation		
__ Poster *or* map		

From *Library Centers* © 1997 Judith A. Sykes. Libraries Unlimited. (800) 237-6124.

TITANIC

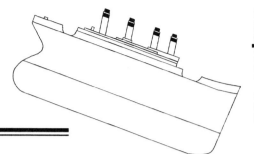

Chapter Ten

Titanic centers are based on a language arts theme for use with upper elementary grades. The *Titanic* can be a particularly motivating and interesting theme. Students are fascinated with the construction of the ship, the idea that it was supposed to be unsinkable, the tragic and heroic human stories, the discovery of the wreckage by scientist Robert Ballard, and the current raising of the hull for the American Titanic Museum. These centers require about 12 hours of library time. Other classes and guests can be invited to culminating events for this theme when the centers are completed.

Students enjoy the novel *A Night to Remember* by Walter Lord, as well as the black-and-white movie of the same name. National Geographic's video on recovering the *Titanic* is interesting to rent or purchase for this theme. As themes develop and continue, you will find many resources to add to your collection.

TITANIC 1

Materials Needed

- Titanic 1 direction cards. (See fig. 10.1, p. 117.)
- Access to Internet and Web sites, if possible.
- Variety of *Titanic*-related materials from vertical files, newspaper archives, picture files, books (if you have a few on the topic; otherwise, the books are needed at another center), public libraries.
- Other sources. (For example, a student's babysitter's grandmother had survived the wreck of the *Titanic* and provided us with her personal memoirs.)
- Poster paper, felt-tip markers, glue, scissors.

Method

Students need to check various sources or Web sites, not only to discover a variety of data but also to begin to explore currency and bias in resources. They will see that some items and facts have differing reports, and they will need assistance with this concept. They will also need help with the exploring and determining when they have a sufficient amount of data to create an interesting poster collage made up of their own artwork, writing, and items printed off the Internet (if you are using it).

TITANIC 2

Materials Needed

- Titanic 2 direction cards. (See fig. 10.2, p. 118.)
- Art supplies: small boxes, scraps of paper, scissors, glue, pastels, crayons (especially black), 8.5" x 11" (or smaller) art paper, plasticine or clay, toothpicks.
- Books, pictures, or posters of scenes related to the *Titanic*.

Method

Set up this center at a table or area where newspaper can be put down and books or pictures mounted for inspiration. If you have a kiln in the school, the students might enjoy using clay instead of plasticine for their *Titanic* models. Etchings work nicely on white cardboard (the kind that often comes in hosiery packages). Students may wish to use pencil, crayons, or paint for their artwork. Items such as shoeboxes can be collected from home. Students may need coaching through their projects and advice on design or detail.

TITANIC 3

Materials Needed

- Titanic 3 direction cards. (See fig. 10.3, p. 119.)
- Question cards for *National Geographic* activities. (See figs. 10.4, 10.5, and 10.6, pp. 120-22.)
- Multiple copies (if possible) of back issues of *National Geographic* magazine; December 1985, December 1986, October 1987.
- Cardboard, game pieces.

Method

National Geographic magazine is a readily available source in most schools or libraries. As we discovered, back issues in multiple copies are also easy to find from parent donations, garage sales, and so on. Its reading level is challenging for elementary students, so this center concentrates on studying pictures and reading picture captions for information. This important skill carries over to other periodicals and sources as well. The center also reinforces the skill of using a dictionary while doing challenging reading. Students have extended this center by using a word processor for the final draft of their sentences and also in creating a board game about the *Titanic*. You may also wish to create center cards based on other sources.

Figure 10.1

1 Poster

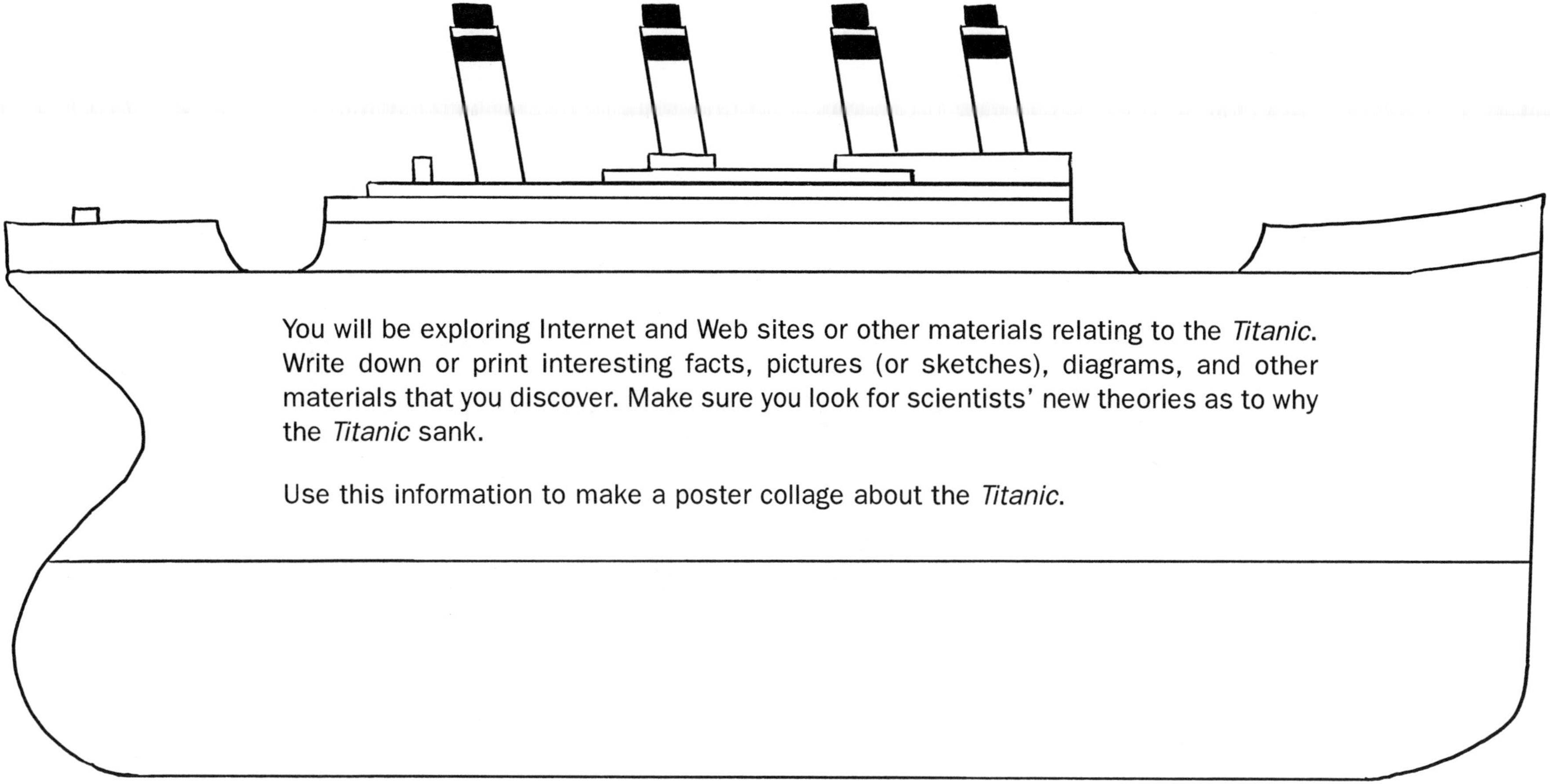

TITANIC

You will be exploring Internet and Web sites or other materials relating to the *Titanic*. Write down or print interesting facts, pictures (or sketches), diagrams, and other materials that you discover. Make sure you look for scientists' new theories as to why the *Titanic* sank.

Use this information to make a poster collage about the *Titanic*.

From *Library Centers*. ∋ 1997 Judith A. Sykes. Libraries Unlimited. (800) 237-6124.

Figure 10.2

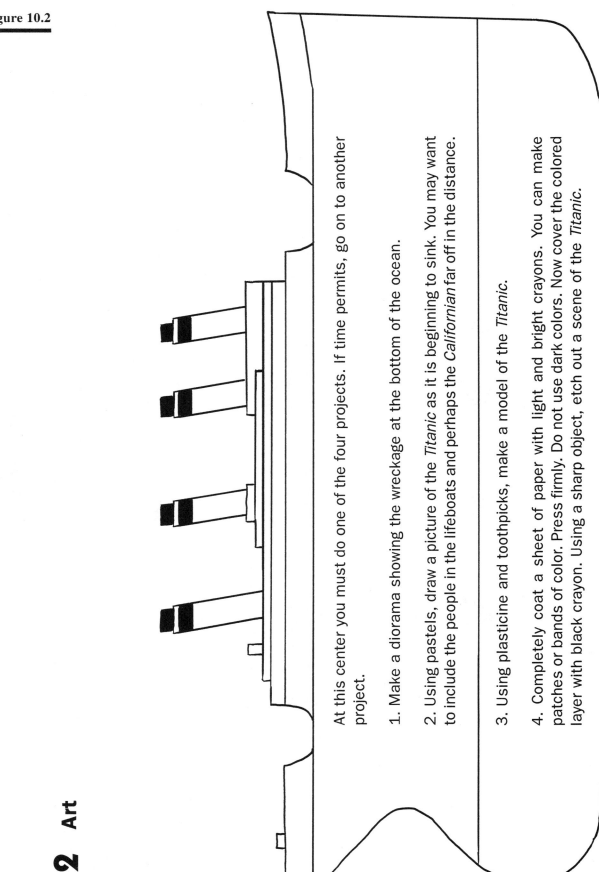

2 Art

TITANIC

At this center you must do one of the four projects. If time permits, go on to another project.

1. Make a diorama showing the wreckage at the bottom of the ocean.

2. Using pastels, draw a picture of the *Titanic* as it is beginning to sink. You may want to include the people in the lifeboats and perhaps the *Californian* far off in the distance.

3. Using plasticine and toothpicks, make a model of the *Titanic*.

4. Completely coat a sheet of paper with light and bright crayons. You can make patches or bands of color. Press firmly. Do not use dark colors. Now cover the colored layer with black crayon. Using a sharp object, etch out a scene of the *Titanic*.

From *Library Centers*. © 1997 Judith A. Sykes. Libraries Unlimited. (800) 237-6124.

Figure 10.3

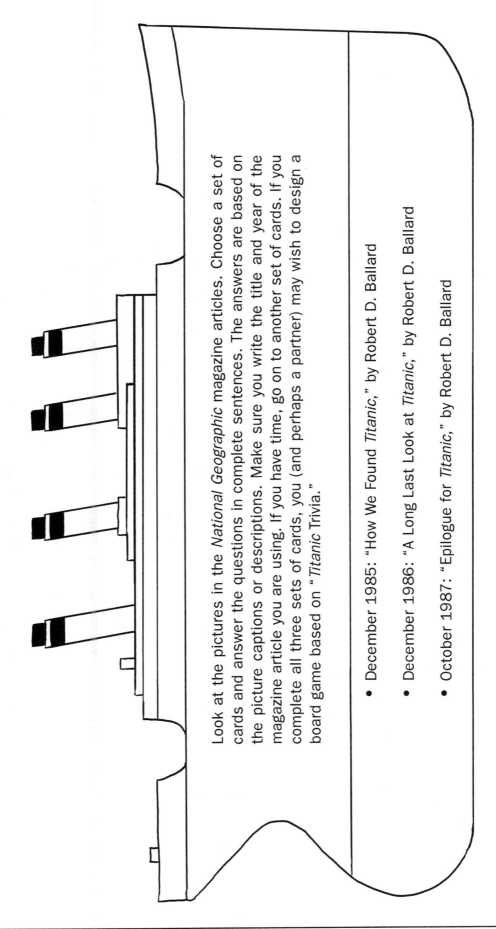

3 Recovery

Look at the pictures in the *National Geographic* magazine articles. Choose a set of cards and answer the questions in complete sentences. The answers are based on the picture captions or descriptions. Make sure you write the title and year of the magazine article you are using. If you have time, go on to another set of cards. If you complete all three sets of cards, you (and perhaps a partner) may wish to design a board game based on "*Titanic* Trivia."

- December 1985: "How We Found *Titanic*," by Robert D. Ballard
- December 1986: "A Long Last Look at *Titanic*," by Robert D. Ballard
- October 1987: "Epilogue for *Titanic*," by Robert D. Ballard

TITANIC

From *Library Centers*. © 1997 Judith A. Sykes. Libraries Unlimited. (800) 237-6124.

Figure 10.4

QUESTION CARD

Use in conjunction with *National Geographic* magazine, December 1985.

1. Page 696.   Study the pictures. Name the chief scientist of the expedition. Name the research ship. At what time was the watch found? At what time did it stop?

2. Pages 704–5.   Study the diagrams that show the events leading up to the disaster. Read about "April 14th, 11:40 p.m." What was the "mystery ship" blocking? What do you think the mystery ship could have been?

3. Pages 706–7.   Find the pictures of the American research vehicle. What is its name? How long does it take this vehicle to reach the wreckage of the *Titanic*? What types of equipment does it carry?

4. Page 709.   What is the object pictured in photo number 8?

5. Page 715.   Name three items shown in the photograph.

6. Page 717.   In picture "L," what is the "bell-shaped" fixture?

7. Page 718.   Name the two survivors in the picture. How old was the woman when she took the trip on the *Titanic*?

8. Page 718.   Name three artifacts on display from the *Titanic* in the photo. What did the initials "R.M.S." stand for?

9. Page 718.   Which museum would you visit if you wished to see the deck chair recovered from the *Titanic*?

10. Page 719.   The photo shows a rescue boat. Describe in a few sentences or a short poem how this photo makes you feel.

From *Library Centers*. © 1997 Judith A. Sykes. Libraries Unlimited. (800) 237-6124.

Figure 10.5

QUESTION CARD

Use in conjunction with *National Geographic* magazine, December 1986.

1. Page 700.   What was the name of the *Titanic's* captain? How many years had he worked on the seas? What was the name of the ship's chief purser? Use your dictionary: what is a "purser"?

2. Page 703.   What was the name of the mother ship used on the expedition to explore the *Titanic*?

3. Page 705.   In the picture, what are the objects that look like stalactites? (If you do not know what a stalactite is, use the dictionary.)

4. Page 706.   How many people can fit into Alvin? What is Jason Jr.? How is Jason Jr. controlled?

5. Pages 709–10.   Find the photograph that shows where the ship separated. Which cabins were located nearby?

6. Pages 714–15.   Identify the objects on these pages that were found on the *Titanic*. Label your answers "a" through "h."

7. Page 716.   Why did the ship's wheel pedestal not rust or corrode like other objects?

8. What are the two objects pictured on page 717?

9. Page 720.   What does the sign on the doorway say in the picture on this page?

10. Page 722.   What was the emblem of the White Star Line? On which object was it found?

11. Page 725.   Where did the statue of the goddess Diana come from? What is the name of the Broadway musical based on survivor Margaret Tobin Brown?

From *Library Centers.* © 1997 Judith A. Sykes. Libraries Unlimited. (800) 237-6124.

Figure 10.6

QUESTION CARD

Use in conjunction with *National Geographic* magazine, October 1987.

1. Poster.   How many separate photographs were used to complete a picture of the *Titanic*'s front section?

2. Poster.   What was the length of the front section of the *Titanic*?

3. Poster.   Describe how the picture on the "mosaic" side makes you feel.

4. Poster.   Name the artist who painted the three small pictures on the back of the poster.

5. Poster.   One of the small paintings on the back of the poster shows the explorer vehicles, Alvin and Jason Jr., resting on the *Titanic*'s bridge. Who spied the iceberg from the bridge, and what did he say?

6. Poster.   Sketch the five diagrams (in order) that show how the *Titanic* sank and broke in half.

7. Page 454.   Look at the artist's painting. What do you think the robot in the painting is doing?

8. Page 463.   When did the *Titanic* sail? When did it sink? When was it found?

9. Page 463.   What was Robert Ballard's hope? What country was the first to disturb the wreckage?

10. Look up the word "Epilogue" in a dictionary and record the definition in your own words. Do you think this was a good title for this article? Why or why not?

TITANIC 4

Materials Needed

- Titanic 4 direction cards. (See fig. 10.7, p. 125.)
- An assortment of picture books or junior books about the *Titanic*.
- Writing paper, word processors if available.

Method

Many interesting books are now available on the *Titanic*. Your library may already have some, or perhaps it can purchase or borrow a few. A good place to start is with books by Robert Ballard. Students will need assistance at this center in story building and editing, especially with incorporating some fact within their fiction.

TITANIC 5

Materials Needed

- Titanic 5 direction cards. (See fig. 10.8, p. 126.)
- Access to a variety of encyclopedias and/or CD-ROMs.
- Word processor, if available.

Method

The most important skill developed in this center is to have students realize that different sources may have differing or varying accounts on a topic. Also, they will discover that an encyclopedia has many interesting articles related to the topic that are not under only the main heading (for example, "icebergs," "SOS"). Students may need assistance with the research process, as well as with the editing of their paragraphs.

TITANIC 6

Materials Needed

- Titanic 6 direction cards. (See fig. 10.9, p. 127.)
- Tape recorder.
- Blank tapes.
- Sound props: anything from a ruler tapped on the table to instruments borrowed from a music room. An area with a sink allows running water to be taped in the background. Sound effect tapes or CDs from the library add effect.

Method

Students usually need assistance during this center to put a script together as a group. They will also need coaching on organizing their ideas, sharing parts, and doing the actual presentation of the script.

Tape recording a radio play

Studying books and pictures

Figure 10.7

4 Creative Writing

At this center you must complete two of the five suggested activities. If you have time, you may go on to an additional activity or create one of your own. Make sure you do a rough draft first, then have it edited.

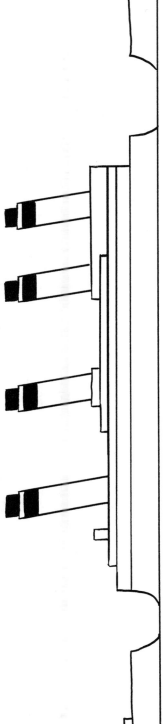

1. Write a letter to a friend telling him or her that you are preparing for a trip on the *Titanic*. Include information about what you plan to pack and why, what you expect on the trip, and anything else you feel is relevant. For your good copy, design your own *Titanic* stationery. (You can make it look antique by immersing the paper in coffee and then letting it dry before you write on it!)

2. Write a diary explaining your feelings and thoughts about your last evening on the *Titanic*. Include information about other people on the ship and what you see happening to them. Perhaps your diary page was found floating in an old bottle!

3. Draw a picture and describe a first-class stateroom.

4. Make a brochure advertising the maiden voyage of the *Titanic*. Draw lots of pictures and show how appealing the *Titanic* was to so many people.

5. Write a story describing what it would have been like as a survivor from the moment you were safely aboard the *Carpathia*.

TITANIC

From *Library Centers* © 1997 Judith A. Sykes. Libraries Unlimited. (800) 237-6124.

Figure 10.8

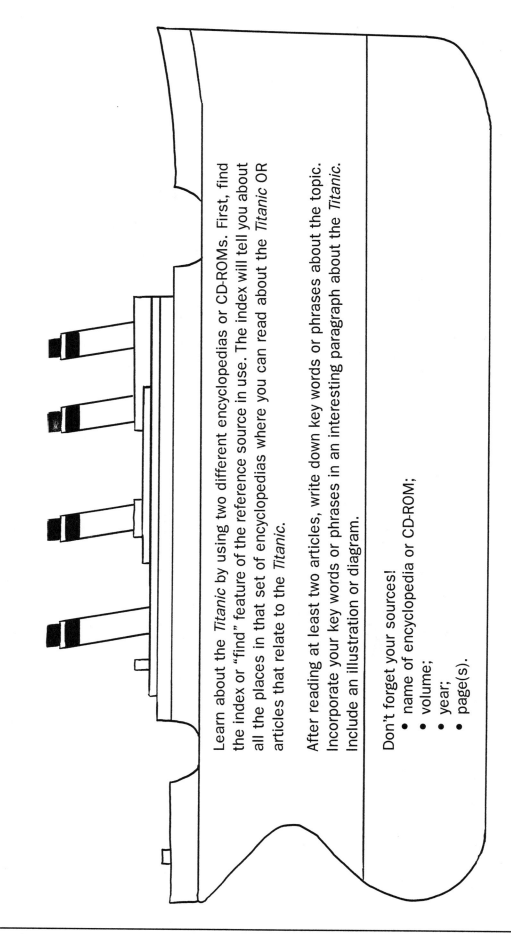

5 Encyclopedias

Learn about the *Titanic* by using two different encyclopedias or CD-ROMs. First, find the index or "find" feature of the reference source in use. The index will tell you about all the places in that set of encyclopedias where you can read about the *Titanic* OR articles that relate to the *Titanic*.

After reading at least two articles, write down key words or phrases about the topic. Incorporate your key words or phrases in an interesting paragraph about the *Titanic*. Include an illustration or diagram.

Don't forget your sources!
- name of encyclopedia or CD-ROM;
- volume;
- year;
- page(s).

TITANIC

Figure 10.9

6 Drama

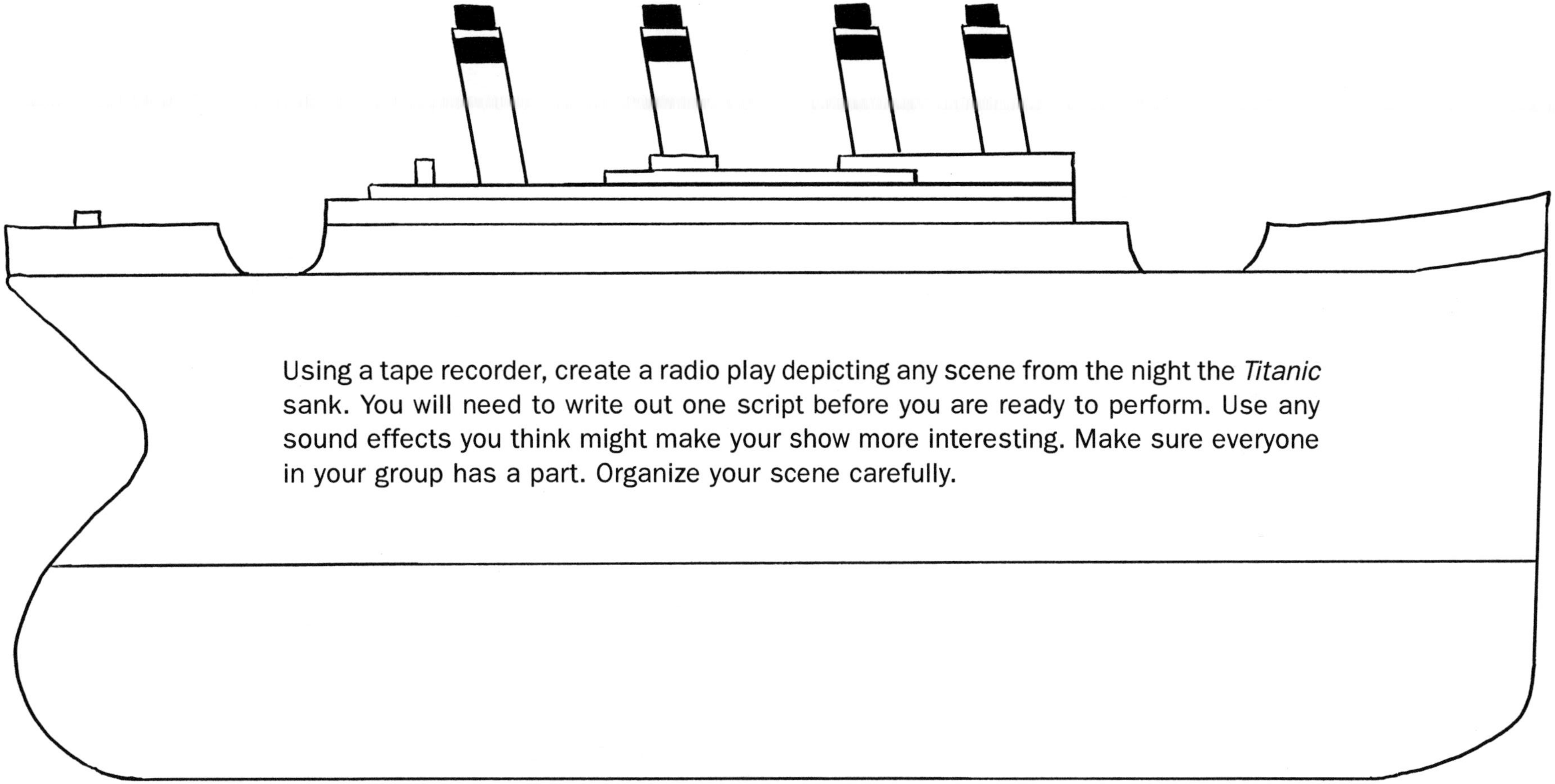

Using a tape recorder, create a radio play depicting any scene from the night the *Titanic* sank. You will need to write out one script before you are ready to perform. Use any sound effects you think might make your show more interesting. Make sure everyone in your group has a part. Organize your scene carefully.

TITANIC

From *Library Centers* © 1997 Judith A. Sykes. Libraries Unlimited. (800) 237-6124.

Figure 10.10

TITANIC
Checklist

Student Name: _____

CENTER	STUDENT COMMENTS	TEACHER COMMENTS
1. "Surfing"		
__ Poster		
2. Art		
__ Project #1		
__ Project #2		
3. Recovering *Titanic*		
__ Card set(s)		
__ Game		
4. Creative Writing		
__ Activity #1		
__ Activity #2		
5. Encyclopedia/CD-ROMs		
__ Paragraph and illustrations		
6. Drama		
__ Script		
__ Recorded play		

128   From *Library Centers*. © 1997 Judith A. Sykes. Libraries Unlimited. (800) 237-6124.

SPACE

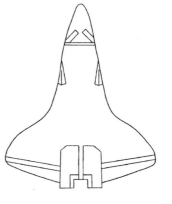

Chapter Eleven

These centers enhance a language arts/science theme for primary students. They could be extended to upper elementary levels with adaptations involving resources and more challenging vocabulary. They incorporate creative writing of science fiction with reading of easy science-fiction books to the students (good ones for this unit include the Commander Toad books by Jane Yolen and *The Trip* by Ezra Jack Keats). Older students could read junior science fiction in relation to the space unit.

The science goals will vary depending on curriculum. The solar system is the primary focus, but the centers extend into other concepts for enrichment. If possible, a visit to a planetarium is an interesting related field trip.

Six centers could be covered in daily library sessions for just over a week, or classes could reserve every second day. Some students may require completion time in the classroom between center sessions. With the primary grades, it is advantageous to have an adult at each center—parent volunteers, university students, school aides, school administrators—whoever is available that week.

SPACE 1

Materials Needed

- Space 1 direction cards. (See fig. 11.1, p. 130.)
- Paper, pencils, crayons, or markers.
- Primary dictionaries.

Method

Students may need some assistance with the brainstorming process while coming up with space-related words. They will also need guidance or reinforcement with dictionary use, depending on how much previous experience they have had with dictionaries.

129

Figure 11.1

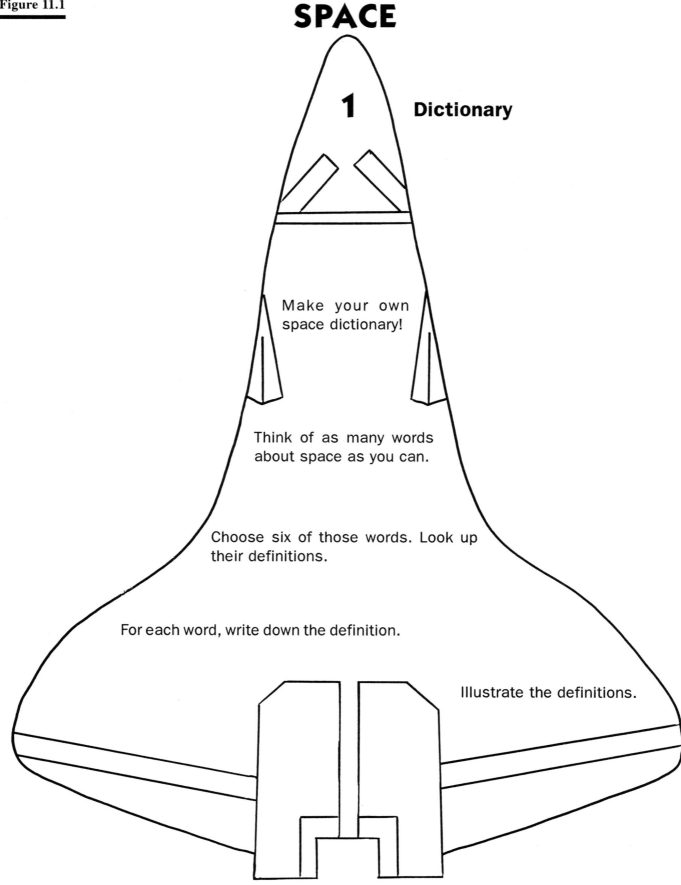

From *Library Centers*. © 1997 Judith A. Sykes. Libraries Unlimited. (800) 237-6124.

SPACE 2

Materials Needed

- Space 2 direction cards. (See fig. 11.2, p. 132.)
- Filmstrip, video, laser disc, or film, from your collection or borrowed. The material should be at primary level on the theme of space, preferably highlighting the solar system.
- Paper, pencils, crayons, or colored pencils.
- Paper cut into comic strip-size strips for cartoons.

Method

In this center, students learn to take notes from an audiovisual source. They may need guidance in discussing key words or choosing concepts to record. Students can learn how to set up a filmstrip or video and to put it away.

SPACE 3

Materials Needed

- Space 3 direction cards. (See fig. 11.3, p. 133.)
- Three sets of 4" x 5" cards, made of colored construction paper. Ideas for the cards: *Set one*—space capsule, star, Mars, orbit, planet, Pluto, astronomy, Moon, Sun, meteor; *Set two*—Venus, astronaut, comet, meteorite, Mars, Jupiter, V-2 rocket, space suit, Moon car, galaxy; *Set three*—Jupiter, Venus, Apollo Space Program, astronaut, comet, spacecraft, galaxy, UFO, Moon, meteor; *Set four*—eclipse, space, planet, Sun, astronomy, gravity, astronaut, Earth, Moon, star.
- A variety of primary encyclopedias such as *Childcraft*, *Let's Discover*, *Compton's Precyclopedia*, *Finding Out*. (Standard encyclopedias such as *World Book* will do as long as an adult is at the center to help with the reading.)
- CD-ROMs such as "Space" or "Encarta."
- Paper, pencils.

Method

Students need an adult helper at the center to assist them in using the indexes or search features to find their topic words. If they work in pairs, they can assist each other in this task and with the reading.

Figure 11.2

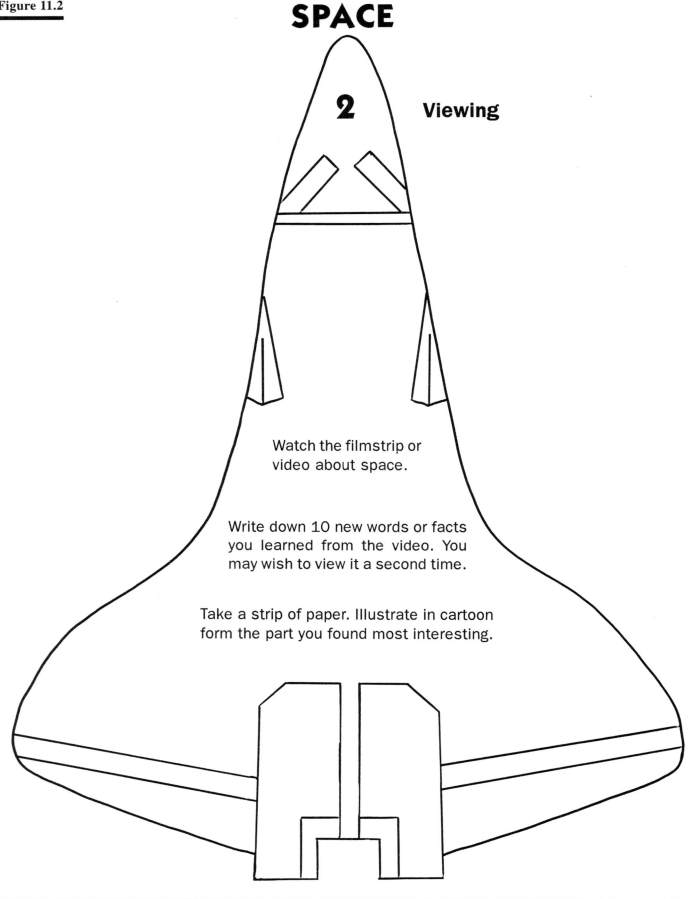

132 From *Library Centers*. © 1997 Judith A. Sykes. Libraries Unlimited. (800) 237-6124.

Figure 11.3

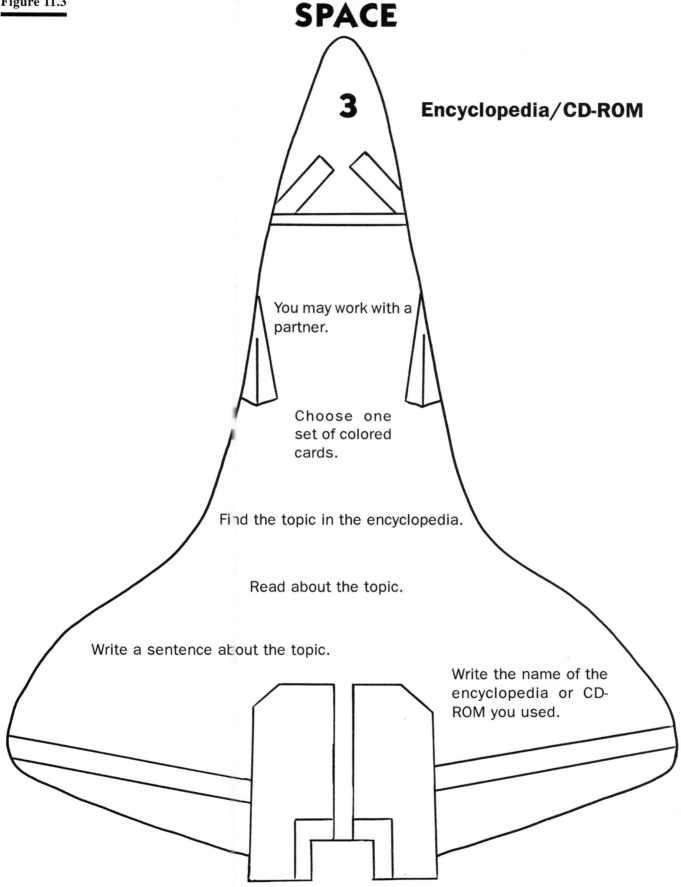

From *Library Centers.* © 1997 Judith A. Sykes. Libraries Unlimited. (800) 237-6124.

SPACE 4

Materials Needed

- Space 4 direction cards. (See fig. 11.4, p. 135.)
- Twelve 4" x 5" cards with space topics listed on them. Draw the topics from titles found in your library collection, such as astronaut, comet, star, satellite, spacecraft, Saturn, other planets, moon, meteor, and so on.
- Paper, pencils.

Method

Students may need to be introduced to or reminded about subject searches in a card or electronic catalog. They will need to know what the call number is and where to find the books. If they finish one card, they should go on to others and try to work more independently.

SPACE 5

Materials Needed

- Space 5 direction cards. (See fig. 11.5, p. 136.)
- Within your collection, or in borrowed resources, find an audiotape related to the planets or other space topics. If such a source is not available, make your own tape by reading from an easy non-fiction book or encyclopedia article.
- Based on your source, create a booklet with three activities:

    #1—Create five closure sentences based on your source; for example, "A path around the sun is called an _____."

    #2—Create five questions based on the tape, such as "Which planet is the largest?"

    #3—Create five true/false questions.
- Pencils, crayons.

Method

Students can learn to set up a tape recorder and earphones. In this center, they practice the skill of listening carefully, to be able to complete the activities. You may wish to add other activities, such as a space puzzle or coloring page, based on the tape.

134

Figure 11.4

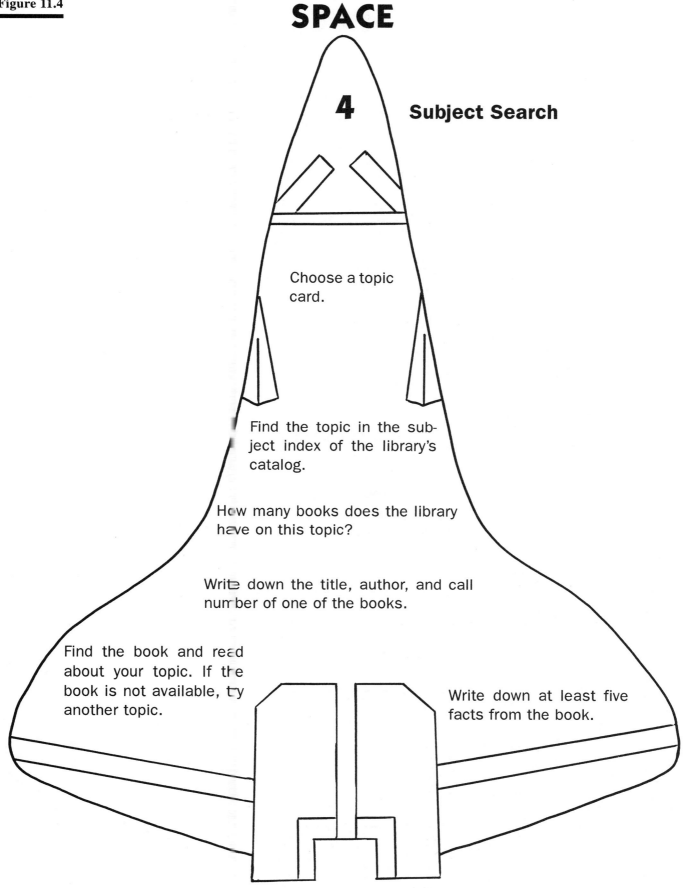

From *Library Centers.* © 1997 Judith A. Sykes. Libraries Unlimited. (800) 237-6124.

Figure 11.5

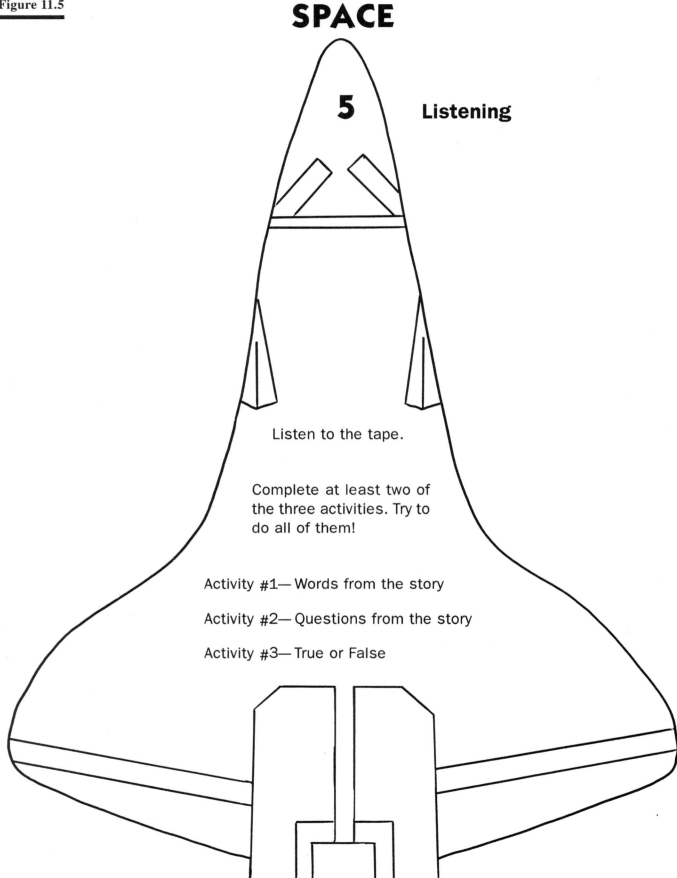

136 From *Library Centers*. © 1997 Judith A. Sykes. Libraries Unlimited. (800) 237-6124.

SPACE 6

Materials Needed

- Space 6 direction cards. (See fig. 11.6, p. 138.)
- A large "space bubble" that covers a writing table. With the class or teaching team, before starting the centers, create this bubble out of two tri-folds (large cardboard display item) placed together, or from large boxes. Students enjoy painting or decorating the bubble in a space theme and painting constellations inside.
- Writing paper, pencils.
- Crayons, colored pencils.

Method

Students will need to be directed in the group activity to discuss a "space adventure." They will then require coaching and editing as they work on their stories.

Figure 11.6

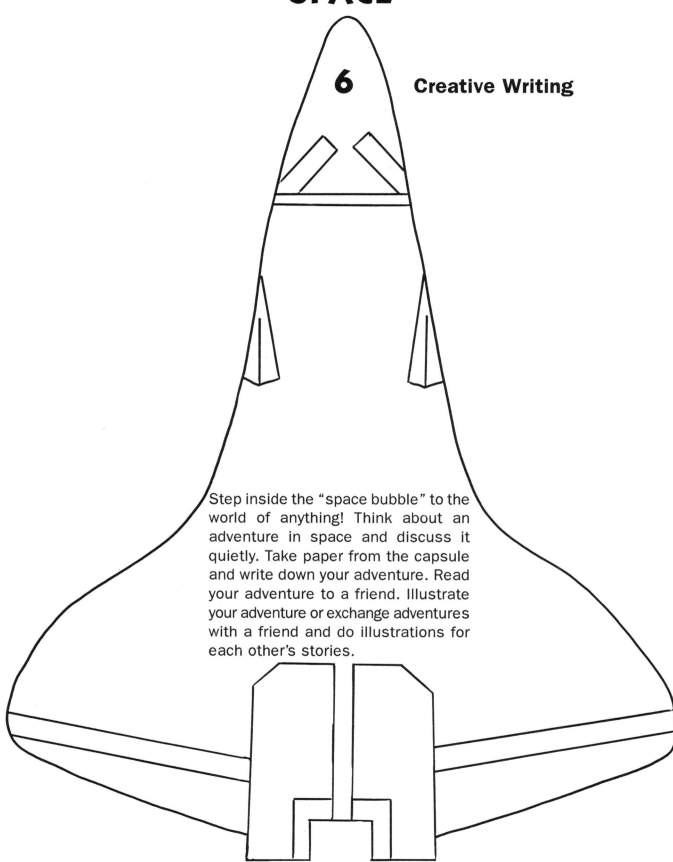

SPACE

6   **Creative Writing**

Step inside the "space bubble" to the world of anything! Think about an adventure in space and discuss it quietly. Take paper from the capsule and write down your adventure. Read your adventure to a friend. Illustrate your adventure or exchange adventures with a friend and do illustrations for each other's stories.

From *Library Centers.* © 1997 Judith A. Sykes. Libraries Unlimited. (800) 237-6124.

NATIVES

Chapter Twelve

These centers enhance a social studies topic—studying a native culture—at a primary level. The centers could, of course, be adapted to other grade levels. Six centers with primary students are usually done six days in a row, in half-hour blocks. Parents or other volunteers may sign up for the centers for this time period. The centers could be introduced with an author study, such as on Paul Goble's Iktomi legends, Tomie dePaola, or another author who writes picture books relating to native folklore.

NATIVES 1

Materials Needed

- Natives 1 direction cards. (See fig. 12.1, p. 140.)
- A video or filmstrip, from your collection or borrowed, on native language. If such a resource is not available, consult books, encyclopedias, the Internet, and local native or aboriginal cultures to make a chart of about 10 words (such as *eagle, hair, eye, bear, horse, moose, head*). Learn to pronounce the words and then make a tape, or tape a local native person pronouncing the words, if possible.
- Matching worksheet with corresponding English and native words.

Method

Students can listen to the tape or watch the videotape and practice saying the native words. The adult at this center can act as a coach here. Students might need help with the matching quiz.

139

Figure 12.1

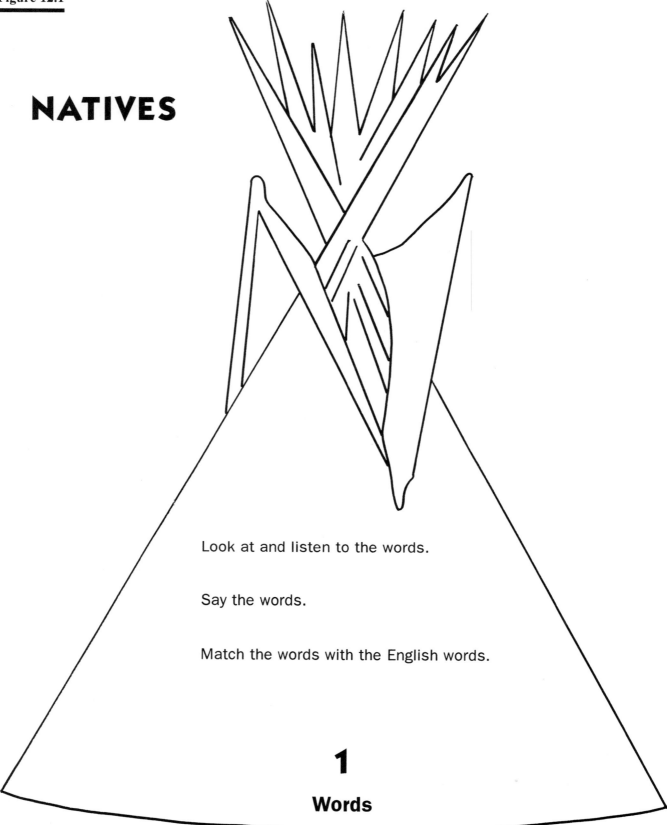

140 From *Library Centers*. © 1997 Judith A. Sykes. Libraries Unlimited. (800) 237-6124.

NATIVES 2

Materials Needed

- Natives 2 direction cards. (See fig. 12.2, p. 142.)
- Large study prints, pictures, and posters dealing with native culture.
- Chart paper for creating large webs.
- Large felt-tip markers.

Method

Students may need guidance initially with forming descriptive words from pictures. At this stage, encourage them to sound out spellings while brainstorming as many words as they can. Some students prefer to do this activity with partners, and they may wish to share some of the webs with the group or class.

NATIVES 3

Materials Needed

- Natives 3 direction cards. (See fig. 12.3, p. 143.)
- Copied sheets with outline of the shelter most common to the culture you are studying (teepee, longhouse, adobe hut, and so on).
- Pencils, crayons, colored pencils, scissors, glue.
- Lids from plastic containers (margarine tubs, washed meat trays) for mounting.
- Items to place around model, such as pebbles, grass, twigs.

Method

Students may need a reminder that many native tribes decorated their homes with symbolic writing that told about family or their cultures. Students can come up with symbols unique to themselves and their families: siblings, a new toy, a pet. They may need some assistance assembling the model.

141

Figure 12.2

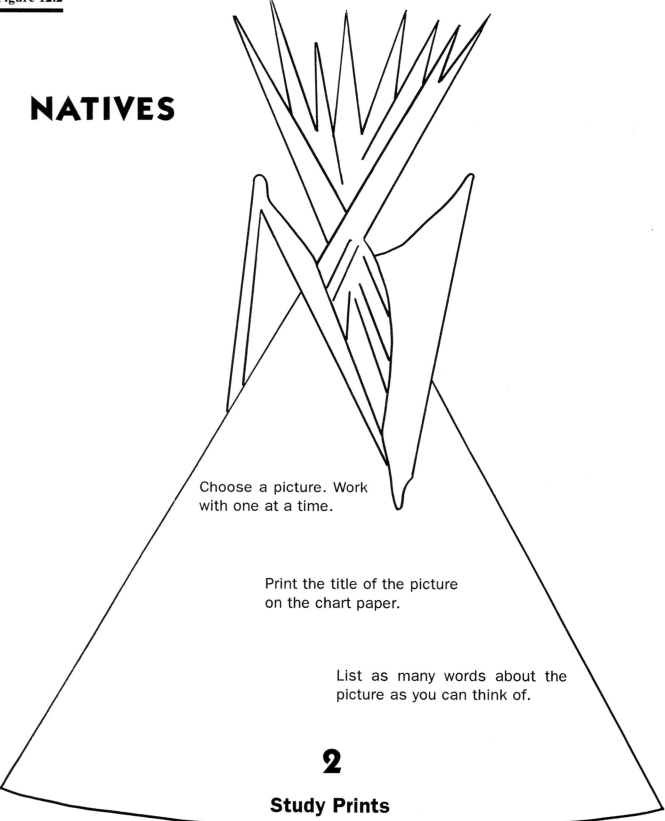

142   From *Library Centers*. © 1997 Judith A. Sykes. Libraries Unlimited. (800) 237-6124.

Figure 12.3

NATIVES

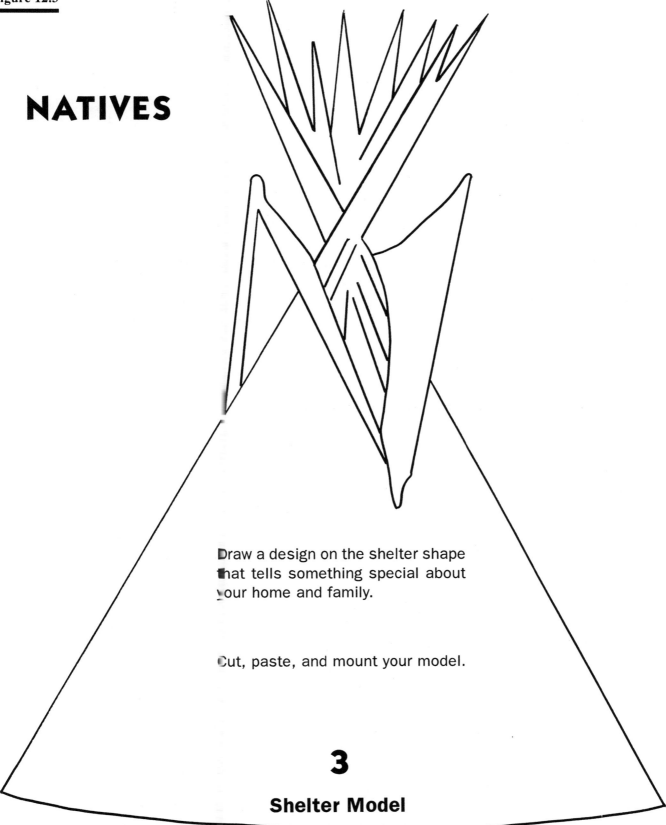

Draw a design on the shelter shape that tells something special about your home and family.

Cut, paste, and mount your model.

3

Shelter Model

From *Library Center*. © 1997 Judith A. Sykes. Libraries Unlimited. (800) 237-6124.

NATIVES 4

Materials Needed

- Natives 4 direction cards. (See fig. 12.4, p. 145.)
- Primary encyclopedias with article(s) on type of shelter corresponding to the culture being studied.
- Paper, pencils, colored pencils.

Method

Once you have selected the appropriate article(s), the volunteer or teacher at the center may read it with the children as a group. If this is not possible, tape-record the reading(s) for the students. Students will need assistance in finding the key words or phrases in the text. If primary encyclopedias are not available, use standard encyclopedias with taped or oral readings, concentrating on using less text. If CD-ROM encyclopedias are available, they could be introduced at this station.

NATIVES 5

Materials Needed

- Natives 5 direction cards. (See fig. 12.5, p. 146.) Fill in the food source pertaining to the culture being studied.
- Encyclopedia/CD-ROM articles relating to the culture's main food source(s).
- Closure worksheet drawn from the article. (See fig. 12.6, p. 147.)
- Puzzle about the food source. Make this by copying a picture of the source, marking it into puzzle pieces, and photocopying it so that students can cut out the pieces and glue them back onto another sheet.
- Paper, scissors, glue.

Method

If a teacher or volunteer is available, you may wish to have him or her read the article(s) to the students. The reading could also be taped. You may choose to let the students explore this topic independently, coaching them in finding an article about the food source and writing down a few key words or phrases rather than doing a closure activity. Remind them to complete the entire puzzle before they start gluing.

Students enjoy preparing or sampling some of the food sources. For example, the teachers or volunteers can have the students help make bannock or bring beef jerky strips in for snacks.

Figure 12.4

NATIVES

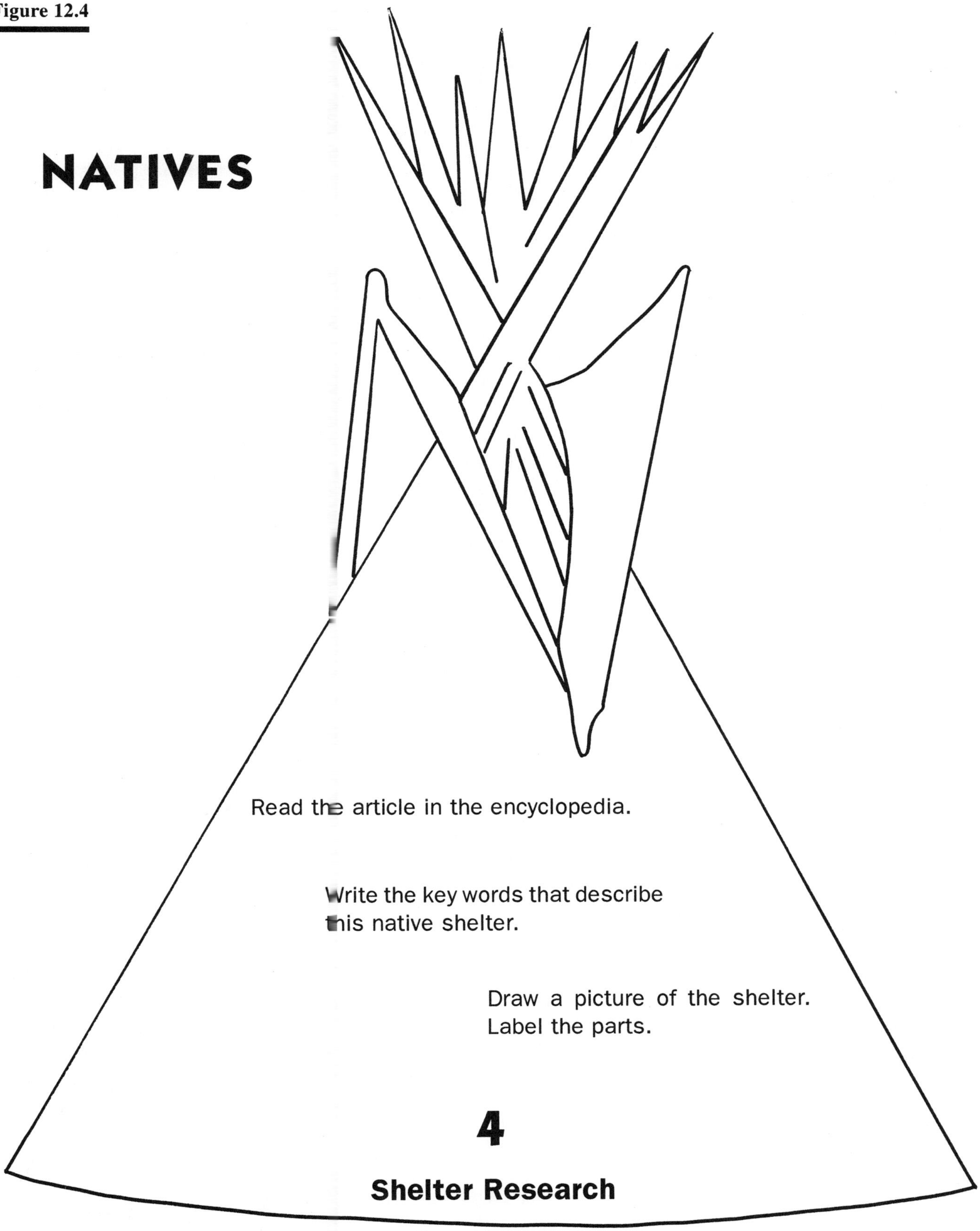

Read the article in the encyclopedia.

Write the key words that describe
this native shelter.

Draw a picture of the shelter.
Label the parts.

4

Shelter Research

From *Library Centers.* © 1997 Judith A. Sykes. Libraries Unlimited. (800) 237-6124.

Figure 12.5

NATIVES

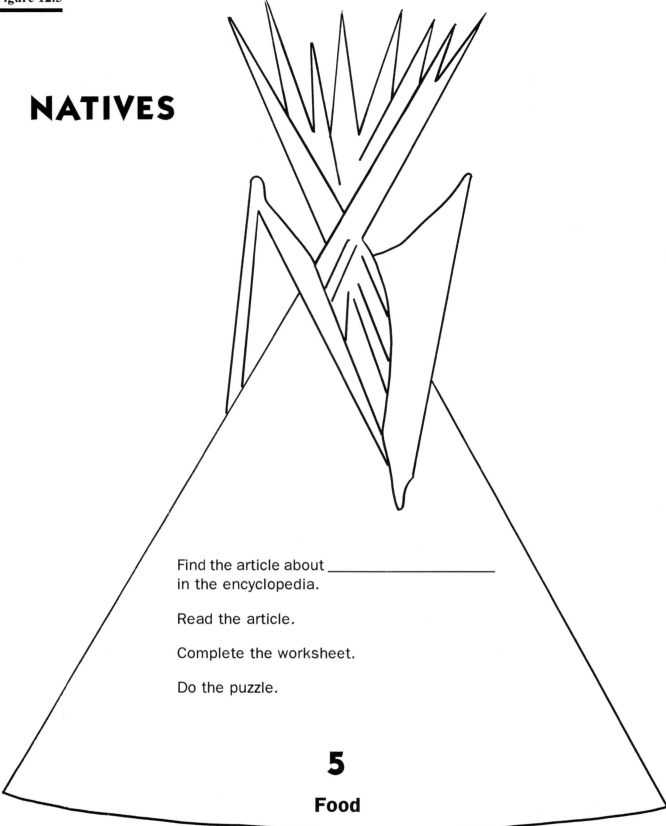

Find the article about _____ in the encyclopedia.

Read the article.

Complete the worksheet.

Do the puzzle.

5

Food

Figure 12.6

NATIVES 5 Sample Closure Activity

"BUFFALO HUNT"

Another name for the buffalo is _____. Its head is very

_____ with _____ horns. It has long

_____ hair and _____ shoulders. It has a

black _____ on its face and a short tail with a _____

at the tip. The Indians used the buffalo for _____ , _____ , and

_____.

From *Library Centers.* © 1997 Judith A. Sykes. Libraries Unlimited. (800) 237-6124.

NATIVES 6

Materials Needed

- Natives 6 direction cards. (See fig. 12.7, p. 148.)
- Books, pictures, charts, and encyclopedia articles, from your collection or borrowed, that show symbols your native culture used for pattern writing.
- Paper, pencils.
- 8.5" x 14" legal paper for scrolls.
- String.

Method

Students may need assistance in writing a few sentences (in English) to tell a simple story; the stories should incorporate words for which there are symbol references. Students then transcribe as much as possible of their stories substituting the symbols for the corresponding English words. They could create a few symbols of their own based on imagining what the natives might have used. For example, if there is not an authentic symbol for rain, they could draw falling droplets. Students may need help rolling and tying their scrolls.

Figure 12.7

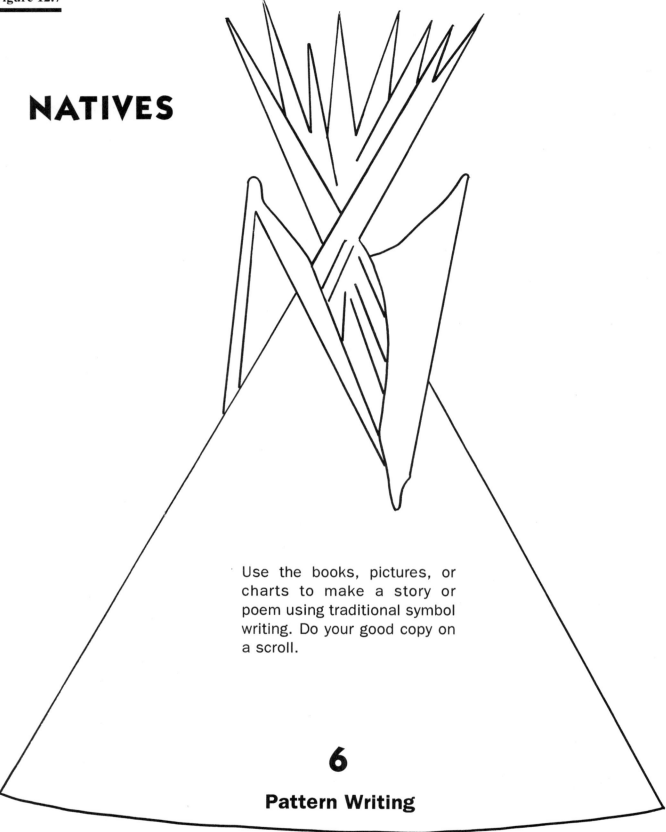

NATIVES

Use the books, pictures, or charts to make a story or poem using traditional symbol writing. Do your good copy on a scroll.

6

Pattern Writing

148 From *Library Centers*. © 1997 Judith A. Sykes. Libraries Unlimited. (800) 237-6124.

NATURAL RESOURCES

Chapter Thirteen

The centers in chapters 13 through 18 were designed to enhance upper elementary social studies topics. First students learn about their province or state, including its natural resources, recent history, and links to other provinces or states. Then students learn about their country: its regions, early history, and links with other countries. They continue to learn about other countries or ancient civilizations through other centers, such as in the "Ancient Greece" units in chapter 9.

Topics such as these often take a teacher a few months to cover in the classroom. The six to eight centers per topic presented in these chapters take approximately two hours each for students in the library; the time can be allotted in a variety of ways. Some teachers prefer to reserve two hours at a time and have the classes do one center per week; others like more concentrated periods, depending on how much time is available and how many other classes are using the facility at the time in the school library program. Some teachers may choose to use only social studies centers, forgoing another type of research project or literature study. Novel studies are often incorporated into a library/social studies unit. Other library skills and processes planned for these centers incorporate several different resource formats and allow students to express meaning in a variety of ways.

Materials for the centers will depend on your collection or what you can easily borrow or purchase. For example, you may have books on wildflowers, or you may have a filmstrip, or you may need to use encyclopedias—the point is to use a variety of resources and formats. Students in the upper elementary grades should be prepared to come to the centers with basic supplies, such as paper (which can be a scribbler or folder with loose-leaf sheets), pencils, erasers, and colored pencils.

The checklist at the end of this chapter (fig. 13.8, p. 161) can assist students with organization, self-assessment, and feedback. It can be used for an interim student report or sent home with the report card.

STATE OR
PROVINCE NATURAL RESOURCES

The natural resources included in these centers are wildflowers, mammals, birds, forests, minerals, mineral fuels, and agriculture. If your area has a unique natural resource, adapt a particular center as applicable. As students move through the projects in the centers, using the variety of materials and media formats, it is hoped that their appreciation for and pride in their state's or province's natural resources will deepen.

NATURAL RESOURCES 1

Materials Needed

- Natural Resources 1 direction cards. (See fig. 13.1, p. 151.)
- Books, pamphlets, and pictures on wildflowers of your state or province.
- Art paper, cut into 4" x 5" squares.
- Hole punch, ribbon or string to tie the mini-books together.
- 8.5" x 11" colorful poster paper.

Method

If books or other reference materials available to you do not indicate which flowers can or cannot be picked, you may want students simply to make mini-books illustrating local wildflowers. You or some of the students may then want to do some research, via the Internet or by writing or telephoning local government agencies or tourist bureaus, to collect this information.

Student letters should be edited. If word processors are available, children may use them for the good drafts. You may then wish to send the letters to your local paper. If you have access to the Internet, you might send them by e-mail; many papers now receive letters to the editor this way.

Figure 13.1

NATURAL RESOURCES

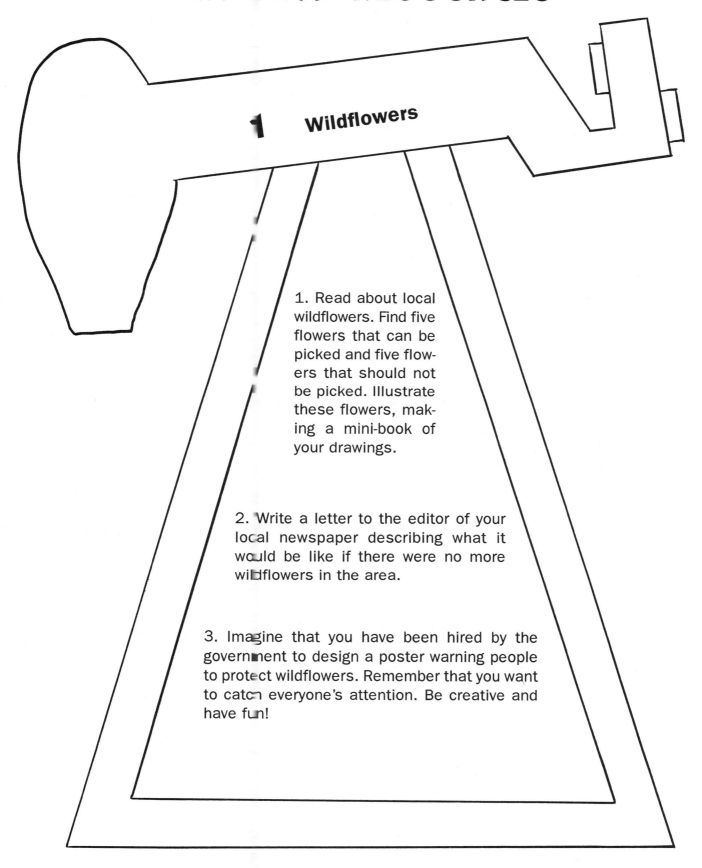

Wildflowers

1. Read about local wildflowers. Find five flowers that can be picked and five flowers that should not be picked. Illustrate these flowers, making a mini-book of your drawings.

2. Write a letter to the editor of your local newspaper describing what it would be like if there were no more wildflowers in the area.

3. Imagine that you have been hired by the government to design a poster warning people to protect wildflowers. Remember that you want to catch everyone's attention. Be creative and have fun!

From *Library Centers.* © 1997 Judith A. Sykes. Libraries Unlimited. (800) 237-6124.

NATURAL RESOURCES 2

Materials Needed

- Natural Resources 2 direction cards. (See fig. 13.2, p. 153.)
- Books or other library materials about local trees.
- Information on pulp mills or sawmills (encyclopedias will have this information).
- 8.5" x 11" white paper to fold in thirds for brochures.

Method

Students may need assistance in locating their information and having their work edited. They will need coaching as they create rebus stories out of reference data. They may need help folding and designing their brochures.

NATURAL RESOURCES 3

Materials Needed

- Natural Resources 3 direction cards. (See fig. 13.3, p. 154.)
- Encyclopedias, CD-ROMs, books, and other library materials on mining and minerals.
- Stencils or word-processing programs (if available) for creating word borders using various fonts and styles.

Method

Students will need assistance in finding information and localizing it from more global sources such as encyclopedias. They will need editing assistance for the paragraph. Some students need coaching to think of sound words from a picture.

152

Figure 13.2

NATURAL RESOURCES

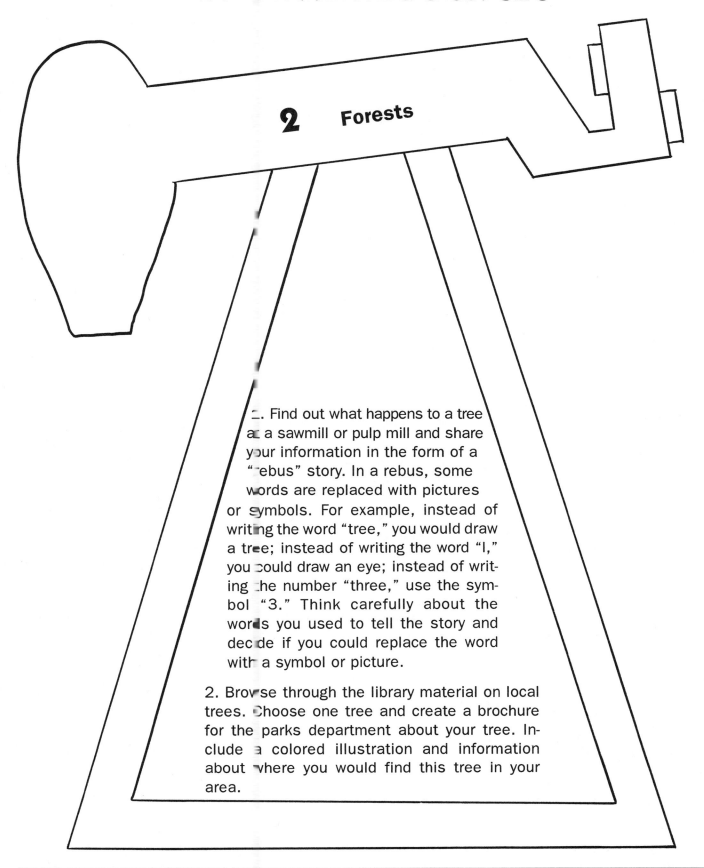

2   Forests

1. Find out what happens to a tree at a sawmill or pulp mill and share your information in the form of a "rebus" story. In a rebus, some words are replaced with pictures or symbols. For example, instead of writing the word "tree," you would draw a tree; instead of writing the word "I," you could draw an eye; instead of writing the number "three," use the symbol "3." Think carefully about the words you used to tell the story and decide if you could replace the word with a symbol or picture.

2. Browse through the library material on local trees. Choose one tree and create a brochure for the parks department about your tree. Include a colored illustration and information about where you would find this tree in your area.

From *Library Centers*. ☉ 1997 Judith A. Sykes. Libraries Unlimited. (800) 237-6124.

Figure 13.3

NATURAL RESOURCES

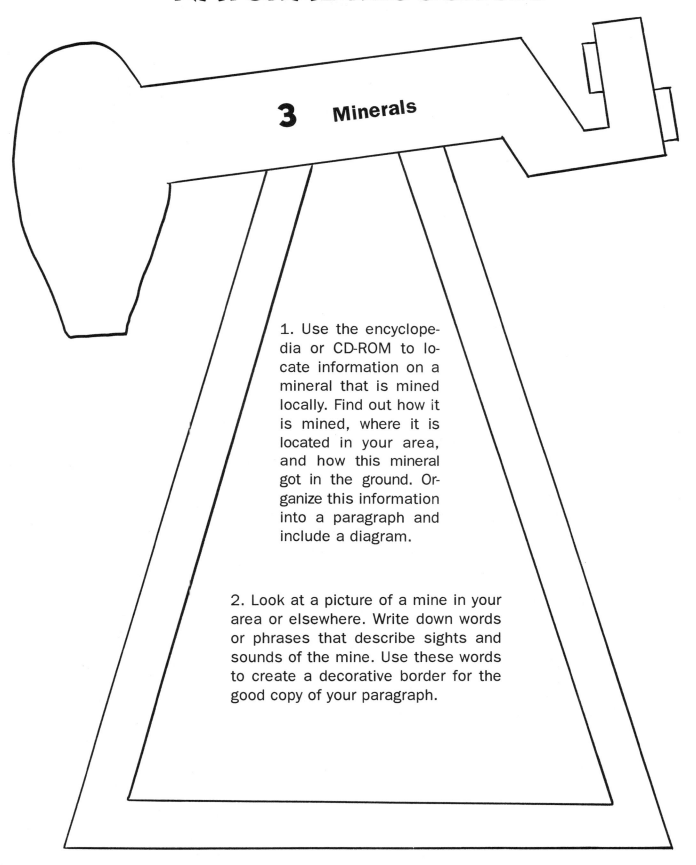

3   Minerals

1. Use the encyclopedia or CD-ROM to locate information on a mineral that is mined locally. Find out how it is mined, where it is located in your area, and how this mineral got in the ground. Organize this information into a paragraph and include a diagram.

2. Look at a picture of a mine in your area or elsewhere. Write down words or phrases that describe sights and sounds of the mine. Use these words to create a decorative border for the good copy of your paragraph.

NATURAL RESOURCES 4

Materials Needed

- Natural Resources 4 direction cards. (See fig. 13.4, p. 156.)
- Encyclopedias, CD-ROMs, books, and other materials your library has on mineral fuels and oil.
- Popsicle sticks, toothpicks, glue, newspaper for the work area.

Method

Students may need assistance in locating the information. Some will need help to understand how oil was formed in the ground. One of the teachers working through the centers may want to take a few moments to explain the findings to the group and give suggestions for the creative drama. For example, the students can start the drama by creatively moving as a favorite dinosaur, then "melting" into the ground or having a volcano in the center portrayed by another student. The third activity, generally a student favorite, may require coaching as to design.

NATURAL RESOURCES 5

Materials Needed

- Natural Resources 5 direction cards. (See fig. 13.5, p. 157.)
- Encyclopedias, CD-ROMs, magazines, Web sites. Magazines are especially good if your library has a good selection of those pertaining to nature.
- Chart with names of local mammals; for example: antelope, badger, black bear, grizzly bear, beaver, bison, bobcat, chipmunk, coyote, deer, Rocky Mountain goat, mountain lion, lynx marmot, moose, muskrat, porcupine, rabbit, raccoon, skunk, squirrel, ground squirrel, wolf, wolverine.

Method

Students will need direction while finding a book, magazine article, or encyclopedia article on their mammal. They may need help finding some of the information categories. Their work will have to be edited.

155

Figure 13.4

NATURAL RESOURCES

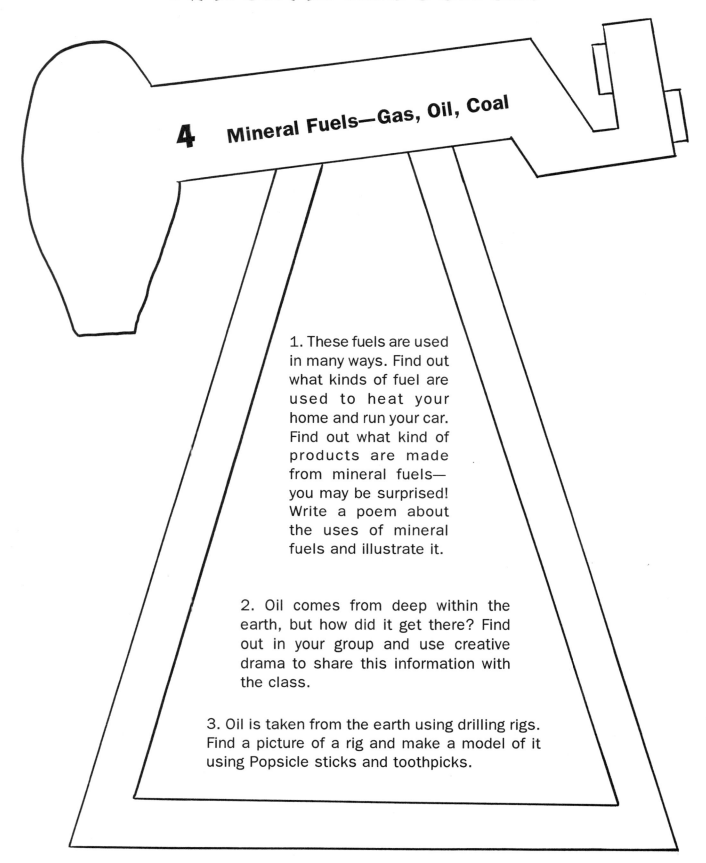

4 Mineral Fuels—Gas, Oil, Coal

1. These fuels are used in many ways. Find out what kinds of fuel are used to heat your home and run your car. Find out what kind of products are made from mineral fuels— you may be surprised! Write a poem about the uses of mineral fuels and illustrate it.

2. Oil comes from deep within the earth, but how did it get there? Find out in your group and use creative drama to share this information with the class.

3. Oil is taken from the earth using drilling rigs. Find a picture of a rig and make a model of it using Popsicle sticks and toothpicks.

From *Library Centers*. © 1997 Judith A. Sykes. Libraries Unlimited. (800) 237-6124.

Figure 13.5

NATURAL RESOURCES

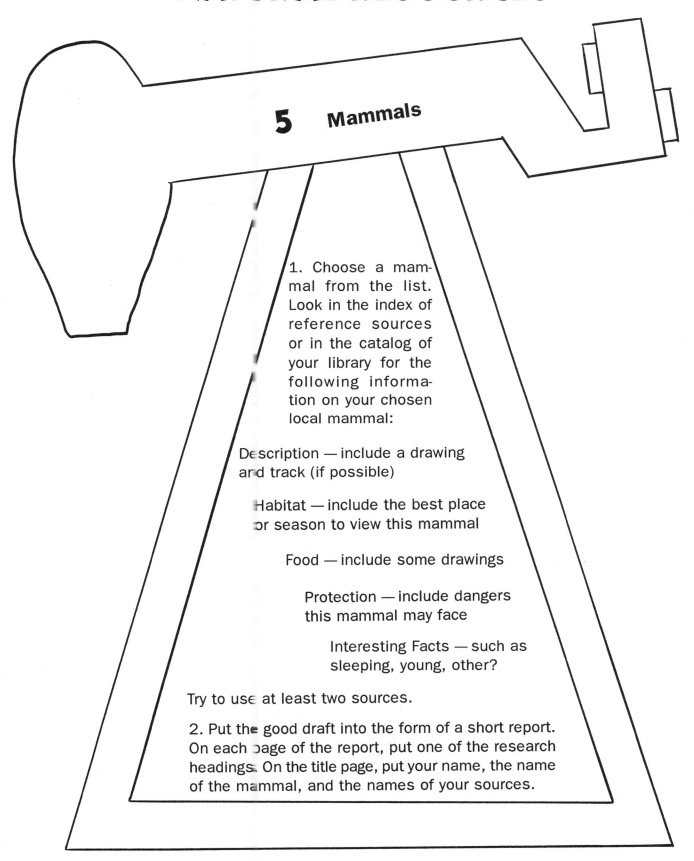

5   Mammals

1. Choose a mammal from the list. Look in the index of reference sources or in the catalog of your library for the following information on your chosen local mammal:

Description — include a drawing and track (if possible)

Habitat — include the best place or season to view this mammal

Food — include some drawings

Protection — include dangers this mammal may face

Interesting Facts — such as sleeping, young, other?

Try to use at least two sources.

2. Put the good draft into the form of a short report. On each page of the report, put one of the research headings. On the title page, put your name, the name of the mammal, and the names of your sources.

From *Library Centers.* © 1997 Judith A. Sykes. Libraries Unlimited. (800) 237-6124.

NATURAL RESOURCES 6

Materials Needed

- Natural Resources 6 direction cards. (See fig. 13.6, p. 159.)
- Books, pamphlets, and other materials on local bird life.
- Word processors for story writing, if available.

Method

Students may need coaching or assistance in locating a bird to write about, as well as in recording pertinent key words or phrases. The challenge this center presents for many students is incorporating fact into fiction. When editing the stories with the students, you may need to suggest areas where they could add facts, for example, in describing the bird they see from the window. The teacher or librarian may wish to share bird literature with the class to prepare the students for this concept; a novel such as Farley Mowat's *Owls in the Family* is a good start.

NATURAL RESOURCES 7

Materials Needed

- Natural Resources 7 direction cards. (See fig. 13.7, p. 160.)
- Books or other reference material on local agriculture.
- Magazines that can be cut up.
- Cardboard for backing (hosiery cards, cereal boxes, and so on).
- Glue, scissors.
- Wire coat hangers (students can bring from home).
- Art paper, watercolor paints if available.

Method

You will need to guide students to charts or graphs referring to state or provincial agriculture. Books or articles often include pictures of agricultural equipment or rural scenes. Some students may need assistance with finding magazine pictures that pertain to the product; for example, if wheat were one of the crops, they could cut out pictures of bread, baking flour, cereal, and so on for their mobiles.

Figure 13.6

NATURAL RESOURCES

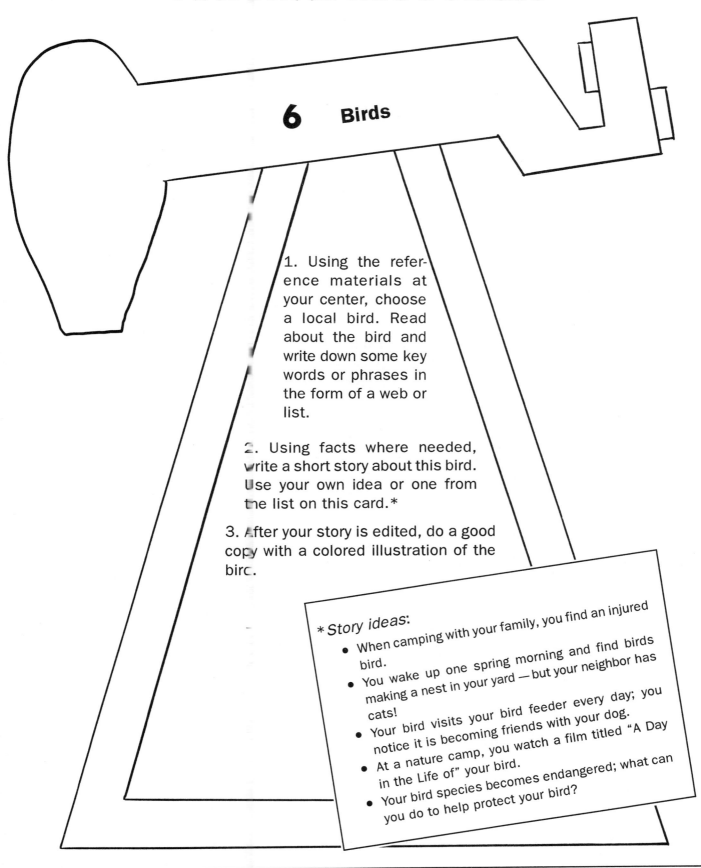

6   Birds

1. Using the reference materials at your center, choose a local bird. Read about the bird and write down some key words or phrases in the form of a web or list.

2. Using facts where needed, write a short story about this bird. Use your own idea or one from the list on this card.*

3. After your story is edited, do a good copy with a colored illustration of the bird.

*Story ideas:
- When camping with your family, you find an injured bird.
- You wake up one spring morning and find birds making a nest in your yard — but your neighbor has cats!
- Your bird visits your bird feeder every day; you notice it is becoming friends with your dog.
- At a nature camp, you watch a film titled "A Day in the Life of" your bird.
- Your bird species becomes endangered; what can you do to help protect your bird?

From *Library Centers* © 1997 Judith A. Sykes. Libraries Unlimited. (800) 237-6124.

Figure 13.7

NATURAL RESOURCES

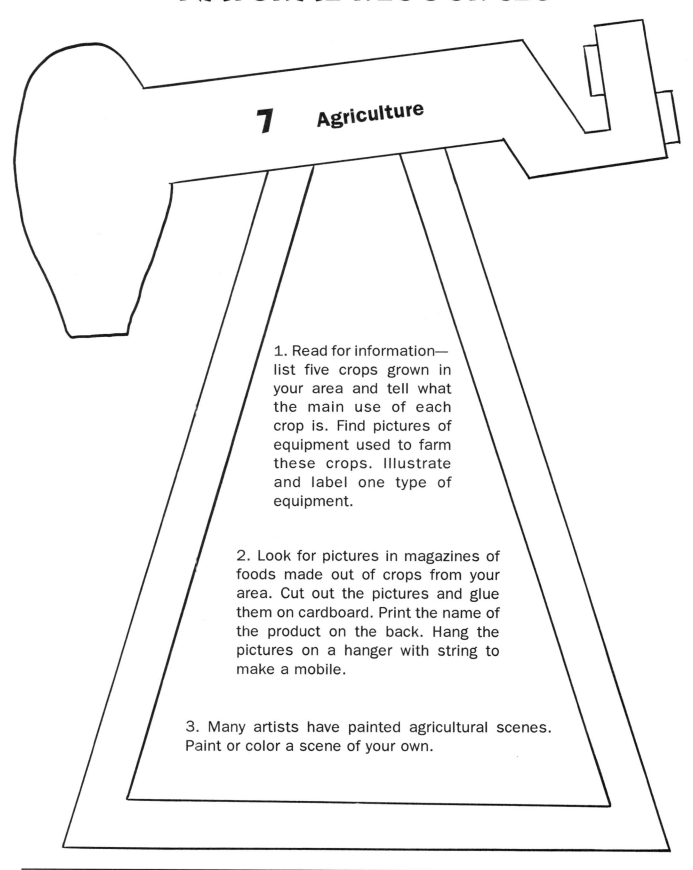

7 Agriculture

1. Read for information—list five crops grown in your area and tell what the main use of each crop is. Find pictures of equipment used to farm these crops. Illustrate and label one type of equipment.

2. Look for pictures in magazines of foods made out of crops from your area. Cut out the pictures and glue them on cardboard. Print the name of the product on the back. Hang the pictures on a hanger with string to make a mobile.

3. Many artists have painted agricultural scenes. Paint or color a scene of your own.

From *Library Centers*. © 1997 Judith A. Sykes. Libraries Unlimited. (800) 237-6124.

Figure 13.8

NATURAL RESOURCES
Checklist

Student Name: _____

When you finish a center, draw a circle around the center's number on this page. Write what you learned and evaluate how you worked. Your teacher(s) will comment, too.

1. My comments: _____

   _____

   Teacher: _____

2. My comments: _____

   _____

   Teacher: _____

3. My comments: _____

   _____

   Teacher: _____

4. My comments: _____

   _____

   Teacher: _____

5. My comments _____

   _____

   Teacher: _____

6. My comments: _____

   _____

   Teacher: _____

7. My comments: _____

   _____

   Teacher: _____

From *Library Center*. © 1997 Judith A. Sykes. Libraries Unlimited. (800) 237-6124.

HISTORY 100

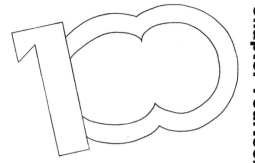

Chapter Fourteen

This chapter enhances the study of recent (the past 100 years) state or provincial history. The centers are themed around world events of the century. Students receive a context as to how those events influenced their state or province. The teacher or teacher-librarian can incorporate novel studies to increase comprehension of world events. For example, Cecia Lottridge's *Ticket to Curlew* or Laura Ingalls Wilder's Little House books are recommended for the settlement years; Bernice Thurman Hunter's Bookie series for the Depression and war years; Eleanor Coerr's *Sadako and the Thousand Paper Cranes* and Lois Lowry's *Number the Stars* for the war years. The characters of these novels (and others) are about the same age as upper elementary students, and through their eyes students can get an enhanced view of the subject eras.

The checklist at the end of this chapter (fig. 14.9, p. 176) can assist students with organization, self-assessment, and feedback. It can be used for an interim student report or sent home with the report card.

HISTORY 100 1

Materials Needed

- History 100 1 direction cards. (See fig. 14.1, p. 165.)
- Books, pictures, posters, and other reference sources showing the types of homes in your state or province built about 100 years ago.
- 8.5" x 11" white paper or art paper.
- Materials for building models of turn of the century homes in your area. You may wish to collect materials for building these models at school. For example, a log cabin can be constructed from rolled-up pieces of brown construction paper, Popsicle sticks, or twigs; a brick house from red plasticine; or a sod house (which is easier for a student to make at home) with bits of grass and dirt.

163

Method

The challenge to students in this center is to discover the advantages or disadvantages of these early houses. Students may need coaching or discussion about reading reference works for this type of information. When labelling their movie sets, they will need to incorporate some of these points. Ask them to imagine that their set crew was building this type of home for real use. For example, if a movie set were to include a sod house, the actors would have to be careful about coping with insects or rainy days.

HISTORY 100 2

Materials Needed

- History 100 2 direction cards. (See fig. 14.2, p. 166.)
- Books, posters, and pictures relating to native figures and artifacts of your state or province from the last 100 years; often encyclopedias have this kind of data.
- Toothpicks, colored 8.5" x 11" construction paper, glue sticks.
- Sketching paper.
- Large (16" x 20") paper for big books, cardboard for cover, felt-tip markers or paints.

Method

Students may need to discuss what an artifact is (for example, contrast a bow and arrow with a teepee). They will need to use the indexes of books or encyclopedias to find the appropriate tribe and pictures of their artifacts. You may wish to check their toothpick designs before they start gluing, reminding them to label. Some students will need encouragement with the portrait drawing or finding a picture of a local native figure from the settlement years. Stories should be edited, and students will need to choose which parts of their text they will balance with a large picture for the big book.

164

Figure 14.1

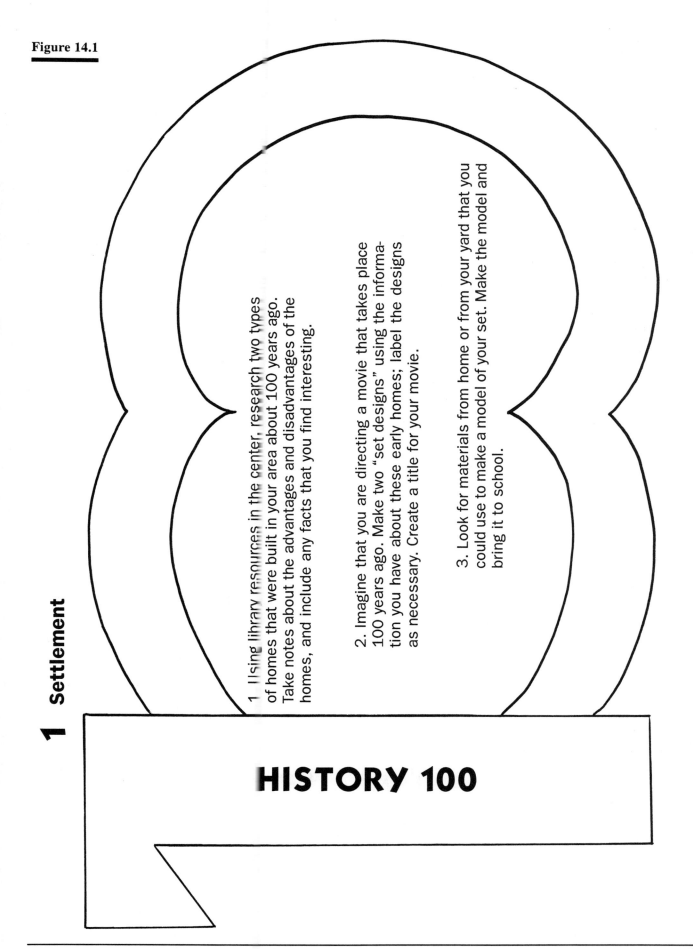

1 Settlement

HISTORY 100

1. Using library resources in the center, research two types of homes that were built in your area about 100 years ago. Take notes about the advantages and disadvantages of the homes, and include any facts that you find interesting.

2. Imagine that you are directing a movie that takes place 100 years ago. Make two "set designs" using the information you have about these early homes; label the designs as necessary. Create a title for your movie.

3. Look for materials from home or from your yard that you could use to make a model of your set. Make the model and bring it to school.

From *Library Centers* © 1997 Judith A. Sykes. Libraries Unlimited. (800) 237-6124.

Figure 14.2

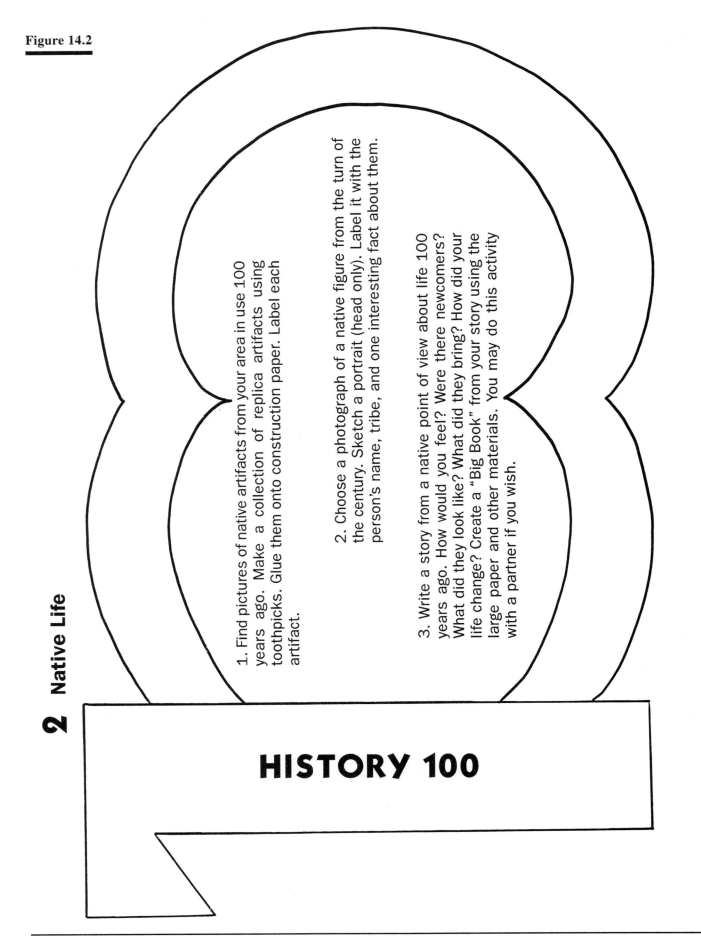

HISTORY 100 3

Materials Needed

- History 100 3 direction cards. (See fig. 14.3, p. 168.)
- Books or other references that direct students to the concept of "making do"; often an article about home-made toys will illustrate it well.
- Photos from books, magazines, vertical file, Web sites, and other resources of your state or province, taken during the Depression years.
- Cardboard or heavy 8.5" x 11" construction paper for game boards.

Method

Some students need assistance in understanding the concept of "making do"—how people used substitute items and made the most of scarce resources. Poems will require editing. Students will need coaching when designing questions for their game. Depending on how much background knowledge they have on the topic, they may need to do further research to create game cards, such as "You lost your job—go back three spaces." Students may want to make or bring pieces to play the games with and share the games with another group or class.

HISTORY 100 4

Materials Needed

- History 100 4 direction cards. (See fig. 14.4, p. 169.)
- List of names of local historical or noted figures from the last 100 years from your state or province. Students can choose a person from this list to research.
- Poster paper and other materials, depending on students' choices of sharing methods.

Method

Students may need assistance at the catalog or in finding cataloged or uncataloged information about their chosen figure. Some will need encouragement or assistance with reading and note-taking, looking for key concepts, and not getting frustrated with too many details. Students may need discussion pointers on choosing how to share their information.

167

Figure 14.3

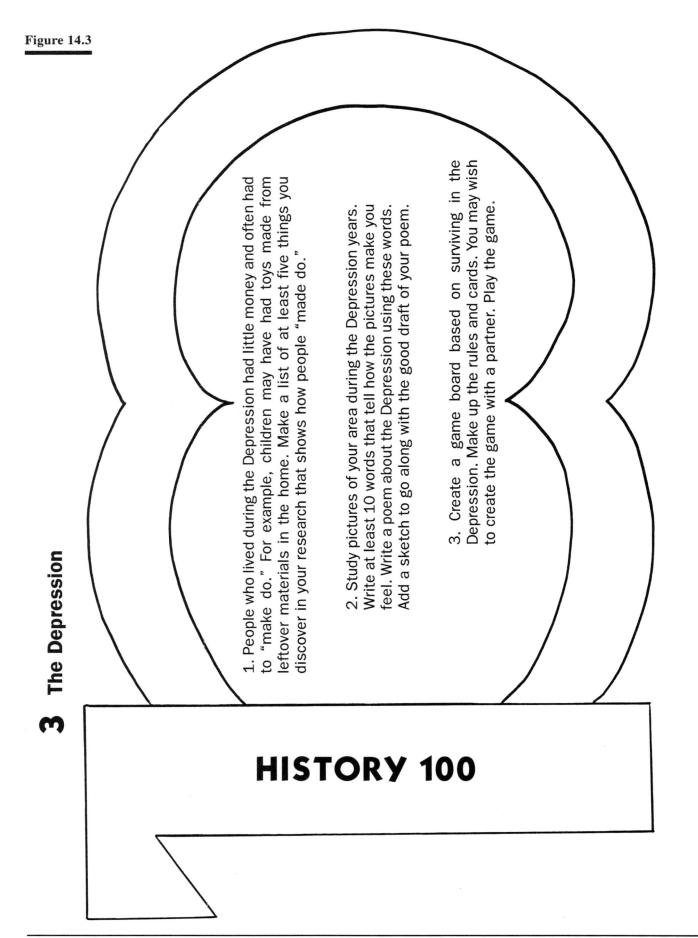

Figure 14.4

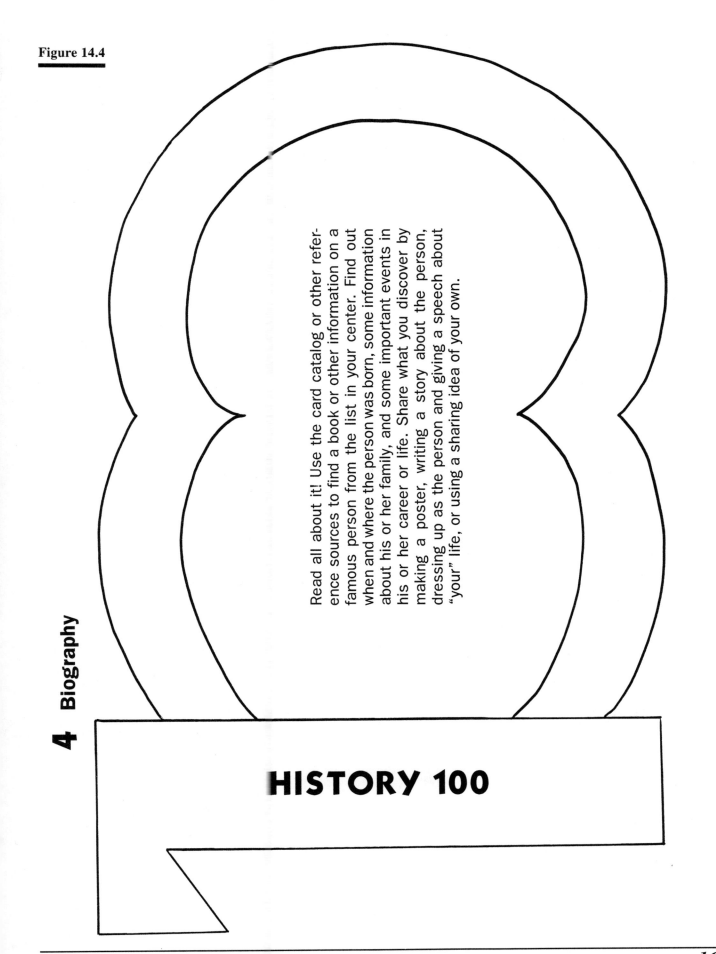

4 Biography

Read all about it! Use the card catalog or other reference sources to find a book or other information on a famous person from the list in your center. Find out when and where the person was born, some information about his or her family, and some important events in his or her career or life. Share what you discover by making a poster, writing a story about the person, dressing up as the person and giving a speech about "your" life, or using a sharing idea of your own.

HISTORY 100

From *Library Centers* © 1997 Judith A. Sykes. Libraries Unlimited. (800) 237-6124.

HISTORY 100 5

Materials Needed

- History 100 5 direction cards. (See fig. 14.5, p. 171.)
- Books or other reference materials on the world wars.
- Patterns for word searches, if available; otherwise, students can make them with rulers on white paper.
- Computer program(s) for designing puzzles, if available. Students can also design their crosswords with paper and pencil.

Method

Students usually find this topic very interesting. Some students may need assistance in narrowing a topic or in understanding certain concepts. Students will also need help with spelling while creating their word puzzles.

HISTORY 100 6

Materials Needed

- History 100 6 direction cards. (See fig. 14.6, p. 172.)
- Dictionary.
- Tapes, tape recorder.
- Pictures of immigrants arriving in your country or area within the last 100 years.

Method

Students will need assistance with finding five immigrants. They can ask others in the group or class if their grandparents or other relatives or neighbors came from other countries. Students in your school who are immigrants often enjoy the chance to be interviewed; you may want to set this up ahead of time or have the students conduct the interviews at recess or after school.

Figure 14.5

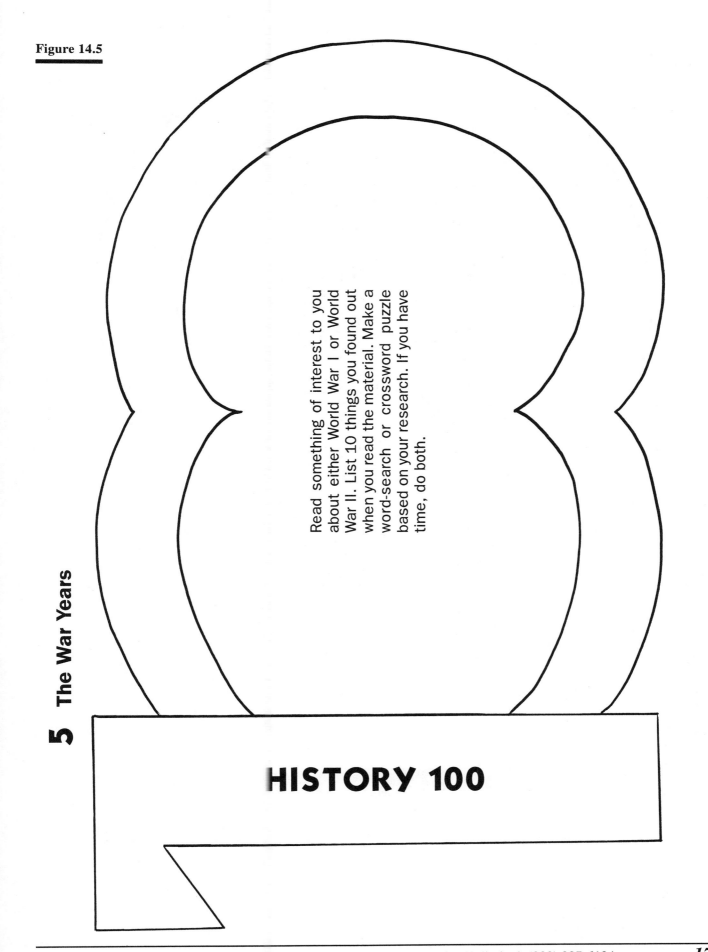

From *Library Centers*. © 1997 Judith A. Sykes. Libraries Unlimited. (800) 237-6124.

Figure 14.6

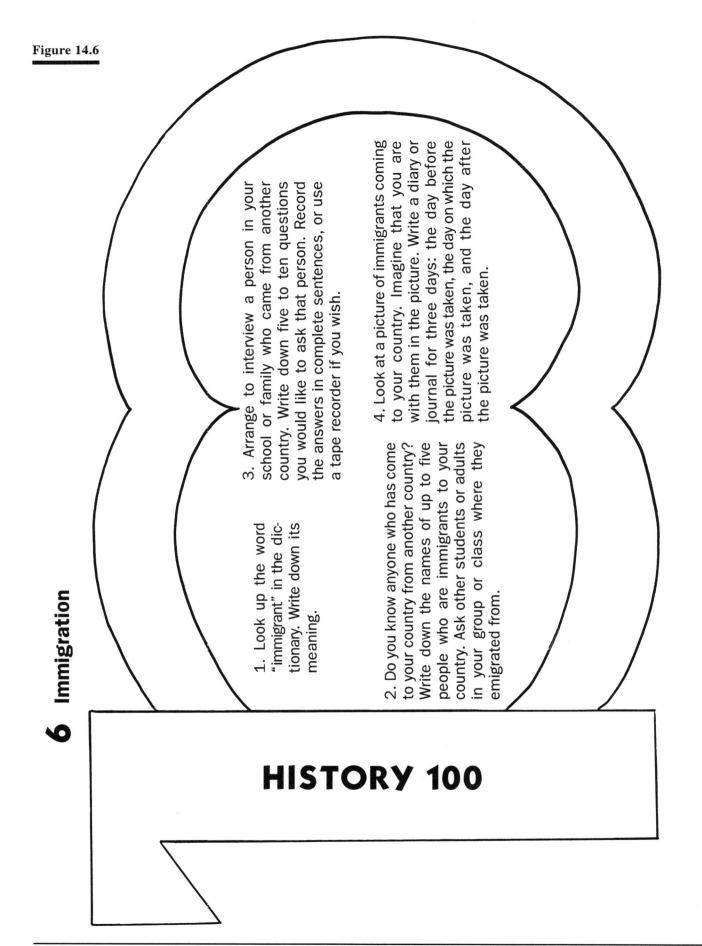

6 Immigration

1. Look up the word "immigrant" in the dictionary. Write down its meaning.

2. Do you know anyone who has come to your country from another country? Write down the names of up to five people who are immigrants to your country. Ask other students or adults in your group or class where they emigrated from.

3. Arrange to interview a person in your school or family who came from another country. Write down five to ten questions you would like to ask that person. Record the answers in complete sentences, or use a tape recorder if you wish.

4. Look at a picture of immigrants coming to your country. Imagine that you are with them in the picture. Write a diary or journal for three days: the day before the picture was taken, the day on which the picture was taken, and the day after the picture was taken.

HISTORY 100

172   From Library Centers. © 1997 Judith A. Sykes. Libraries Unlimited. (800) 237-6124.

HISTORY 100 7

Materials Needed

- History 100 7 direct on cards. (See fig. 14.7, p. 174.)
- Bound catalogs from earlier eras. These can often be found in library collections; if you do not have any, you may need to borrow from another source, although encyclopedias may have some of this information. Ideally the old catalogs should be from 1900–1930, but if not available use catalogs dating back at least 10 years.
- New catalogs.
- Drawing paper.

Method

Students enjoy looking through "pages from the past" and usually can find items that interest them fairly easily. They may need assistance with finding similar counterparts in a modern catalog. The best catalogs to use are ones from large department stores.

HISTORY 100 8

Materials Needed

- History 100 8 direction cards. (See fig. 14.8, p. 175.)
- Travel brochures from your state or province tourist bureaus or chambers of commerce.
- Books, Internet, or other materials with pictures of local tourist attractions.
- White paper.

Method

Students will need help at certain points with their creative designs, especially in adding detailed descriptions to their brochures. If word processors are available, students may want to do the written portion of their designs on computer.

173

Figure 14.7

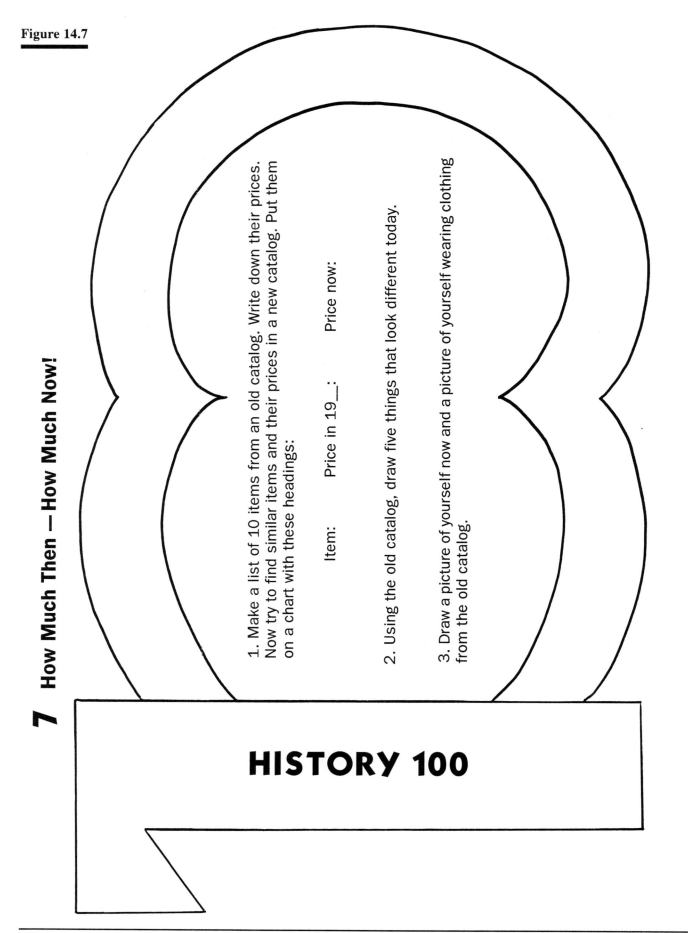

Figure 14.8

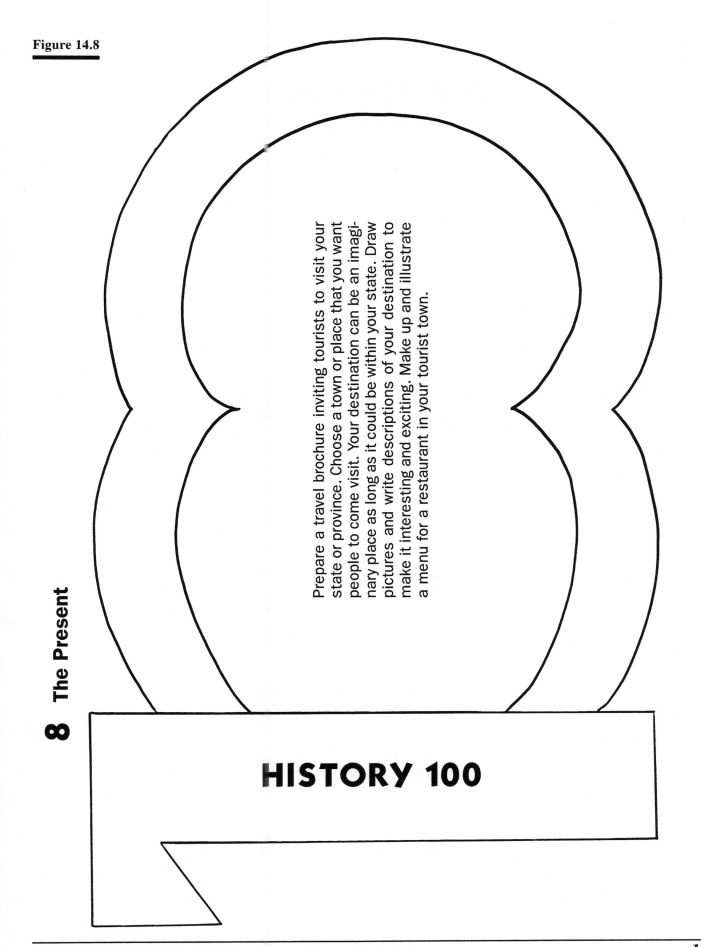

8 The Present

Prepare a travel brochure inviting tourists to visit your state or province. Choose a town or place that you want people to come visit. Your destination can be an imaginary place as long as it could be within your state. Draw pictures and write descriptions of your destination to make it interesting and exciting. Make up and illustrate a menu for a restaurant in your tourist town.

HISTORY 100

From *Library Centers*. © 1997 Judith A. Sykes. Libraries Unlimited. (800) 237-6124.

Figure 14.9

HISTORY 100
Checklist

Student Name: _____

When you finish a center, circle the number of the center on this page. Write what you learned and evaluate how you worked. Your teacher(s) will comment as well.

1. My comments: _____

   _____

   Teacher:_____

2. My comments: _____

   _____

   Teacher:_____

3. My comments: _____

   _____

   Teacher:_____

4. My comments: _____

   _____

   Teacher:_____

5. My comments: _____

   _____

   Teacher:_____

6. My comments: _____

   _____

   Teacher:_____

7. My comments: _____

   _____

   Teacher:_____

8. My comments: _____

   _____

   Teacher:_____

176   From *Library Centers*. © 1997 Judith A. Sykes. Libraries Unlimited. (800) 237-6124.

LINKS WITHIN BORDERS

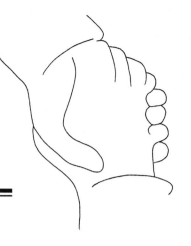

Chapter Fifteen

These centers enhance a study of interdependence, within a country, between two states or provinces. When choosing another state or province to study, consider an area that is culturally or geographically different from your area. Perhaps the contrasted area uses a different language, such as Spanish or French. Use the Internet or other mode of communication to engage your students with penpals from the chosen state or province, if possible.

The checklist at the end of this chapter (fig. 15.8, p. 188) can assist students with organization, self-assessment, and feedback. It can be used for an interim student report or sent home with the report card.

LINKS WITHIN BORDERS 1

Materials Needed

- Links Within Borders 1 direction cards. (See fig. 15.1, p. 178.)
- Outline maps of the country.
- Atlases/CD-ROM atlases.
- 14" x 20" white or cream poster paper.

Method

Students may need assistance in locating information in an atlas. Some will need encouragement with their motor and art skills when drawing outlines of large maps on large paper.

177

Figure 15.1

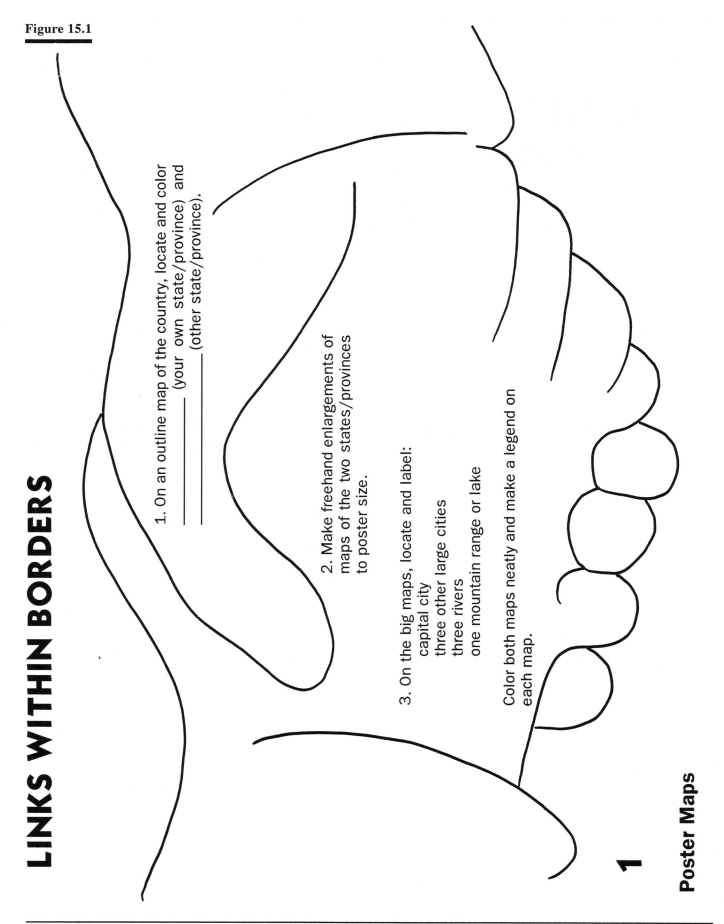

LINKS WITHIN BORDERS

1. On an outline map of the country, locate and color _____ (your own state/province) and _____ (other state/province).

2. Make freehand enlargements of maps of the two states/provinces to poster size.

3. On the big maps, locate and label:
   capital city
   three other large cities
   three rivers
   one mountain range or lake

Color both maps neatly and make a legend on each map.

1

Poster Maps

LINKS WITHIN BORDERS 2

Materials Needed

- Links Within Borders 2 direction cards. (See fig. 15.2, p. 180.)
- Sports books, periodicals such as *Sports Illustrated for Kids*, almanacs, newspaper articles, Web sites.
- Team rosters and other team information; available on the Internet or by writing to teams.
- Poster paper, letter stencils or computer fonts, felt-tip markers.
- Scissors for cutting out banners.

Method

Students find this center highly motivating but do require assistance in locating information. Some students may be unfamiliar with finding information in an almanac, periodical, or other current source. Access to word processors or the Internet helps a great deal with this activity.

LINKS WITHIN BORDERS 3

Materials Needed

- Links Within Borders 3 direction cards. (See fig. 15.3, p. 181.)
- Books, pictures, encyclopedias, CD-ROMs, Web sites.
- Travel brochures about the two states or provinces.
- White 8.5" x 11" paper folded into thirds to resemble a brochure.

Method

Students need to take key information from the sources regarding the topic of tourism—what to see and do—in each area. They need to be able to describe the event or attraction and illustrate it. They should be encouraged to mention a number of items in their brochures, but also to narrow the topic and choose what they will highlight.

Figure 15.2

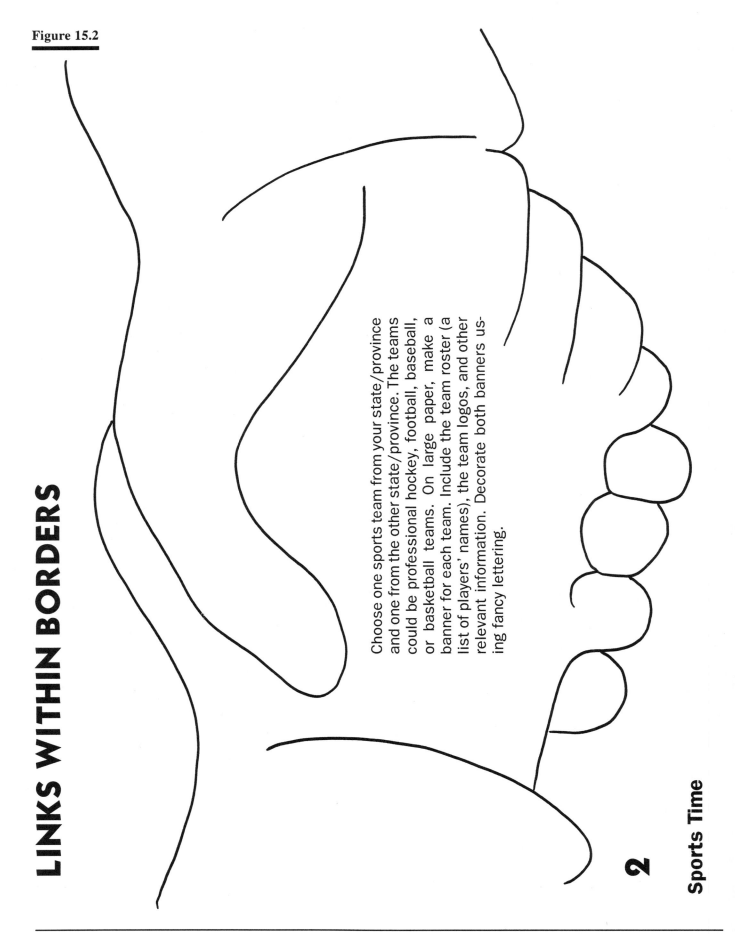

LINKS WITHIN BORDERS

Choose one sports team from your state/province and one from the other state/province. The teams could be professional hockey, football, baseball, or basketball teams. On large paper, make a banner for each team. Include the team roster (a list of players' names), the team logos, and other relevant information. Decorate both banners using fancy lettering.

2

Sports Time

180   From *Library Centers*. © 1997 Judith A. Sykes. Libraries Unlimited. (800) 237-6124.

Figure 15.3

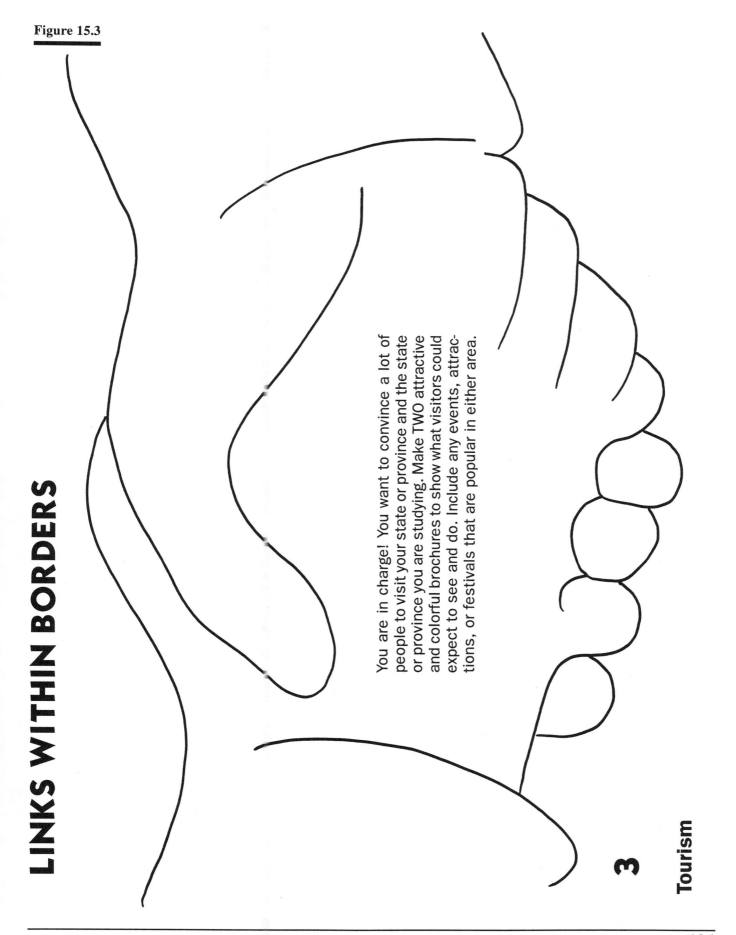

LINKS WITHIN BORDERS

You are in charge! You want to convince a lot of people to visit your state or province and the state or province you are studying. Make TWO attractive and colorful brochures to show what visitors could expect to see and do. Include any events, attractions, or festivals that are popular in either area.

3

Tourism

From *Library Centers*. © 1997 Judith A. Sykes. Libraries Unlimited. (800) 237-6124.

LINKS WITHIN BORDERS 4

Materials Needed

- Links Within Borders 4 direction cards. (See fig. 15.4, p. 183.)
- Books, posters, videos, and other materials pertaining to the applicable food industries.
- Cookbooks or magazines.
- Paper suitable for making menus.

Method

Based on your collection and locale, choose a predominant food industry for which you can provide reference materials. For example, in a study of Alberta and Quebec, "sugar" was a common product (sugar beets and maple sugar). Students created menus for a "Maple Cafe." In Hawaii, pineapple could be chosen; in Montana, beef; in Idaho, potatoes; and so on.

Students might need assistance in locating data as to how the product is grown, picked, canned, or otherwise processed. Encyclopedias and CD-ROMs are usually a good choice here. Your library may have other materials on the subject as well. Most cookbook sections or children's cookbooks have wide-ranging recipes and should include some that use the food products being studied. Donated or borrowed cookbooks or family magazines are also good recipe sources, as is writing to or telephoning the food factories. They are often happy to send out recipe brochures and information on their products.

For the menu, students need only write the title of the recipe (such as Maple Tarts, Maple Ice Cream, or the like); they do not have to copy the whole recipe unless the group wants to prepare it.

LINKS WITHIN BORDERS 5

Materials Needed

- Links Within Borders 5 direction cards. (See fig. 15.5, p. 184.)
- Multilingual dictionaries: Spanish/English, French/English, Chinese/English; whatever you have in your collection or can easily borrow or purchase, depending on your locale.
- Empty cereal boxes, paper to glue over them, glue.

Method

Students enjoy creating a cereal, such as "Maple Crunchies," but will need assistance using the bilingual dictionaries. The French or Spanish dictionaries are usually standard, but if your area or the area you are studying has another predominant language or culture you may want to borrow materials pertaining to that language. Students may need assistance in going beyond their titles to describe the cereals using slogans.

Figure 15.4

LINKS WITHIN BORDERS

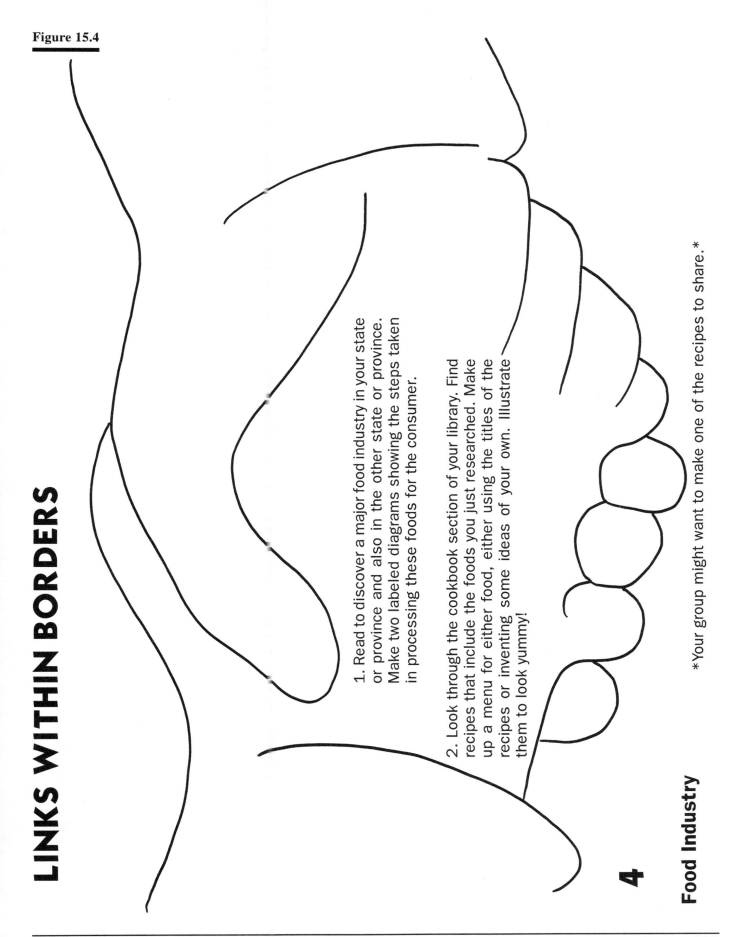

1. Read to discover a major food industry in your state or province and also in the other state or province. Make two labeled diagrams showing the steps taken in processing these foods for the consumer.

2. Look through the cookbook section of your library. Find recipes that include the foods you just researched. Make up a menu for either food, either using the titles of the recipes or inventing some ideas of your own. Illustrate them to look yummy!

Your group might want to make one of the recipes to share.

4

Food Industry

From *Library Centers*. © 1997 Judith A. Sykes. Libraries Unlimited. (800) 237-6124.

Figure 15.5

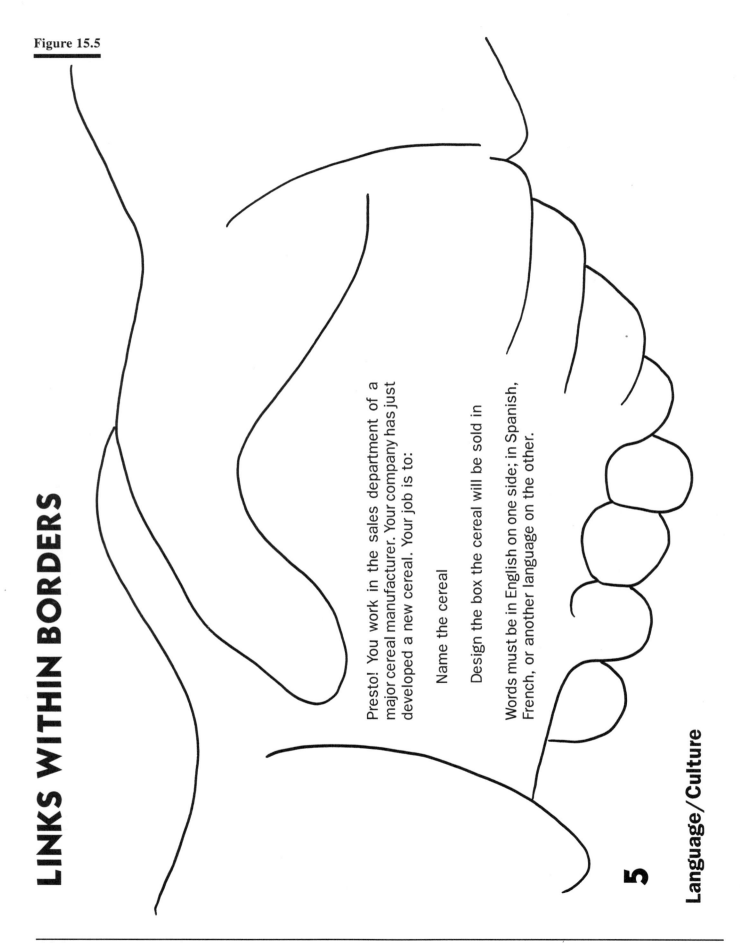

LINKS WITHIN BORDERS

Presto! You work in the sales department of a major cereal manufacturer. Your company has just developed a new cereal. Your job is to:

Name the cereal

Design the box the cereal will be sold in

Words must be in English on one side; in Spanish, French, or another language on the other.

5

Language/Culture

LINKS WITHIN BORDERS 6

Materials Needed

- Links Within Borders 6 direction cards. (See fig. 15.6, p. 186.)
- Books, articles, and brochures pertaining to the two states/provinces in the study.
- Blank audio- or videotape, if the students wish to present their scripts this way.
- Two discarded or toy telephones to use as props.

Method

Students will need assistance with adding factual information to their scripts, especially if they haven't been to many of the other centers or are just beginning the study. They can usually create interesting dialogue or banter but need encouragement to look through the materials at the center to find data to talk about in the scripts. They will need to rehearse and might need assistance with audio- or videotaping. You may want to set up a section of the library for this purpose if you have not already done so.

LINKS WITHIN BORDERS 7

Materials Needed

- Links Within Borders 7 direction cards. (See fig. 15.7, p. 187.)
- Encyclopedias often have "fast facts" with pictures in articles or entries on states/provinces.
- Books and other reference materials on your state or province.
- 8.5" x 11" white paper.

Method

Students may need assistance in locating information. Students will need encouragement for freehand drawing of the symbols. Some state or provincial symbols are quite complex; the idea is not to have them perfect in detail but to have the students make basic, neat outlines or drawings to the best of their ability.

Figure 15.6

LINKS WITHIN BORDERS

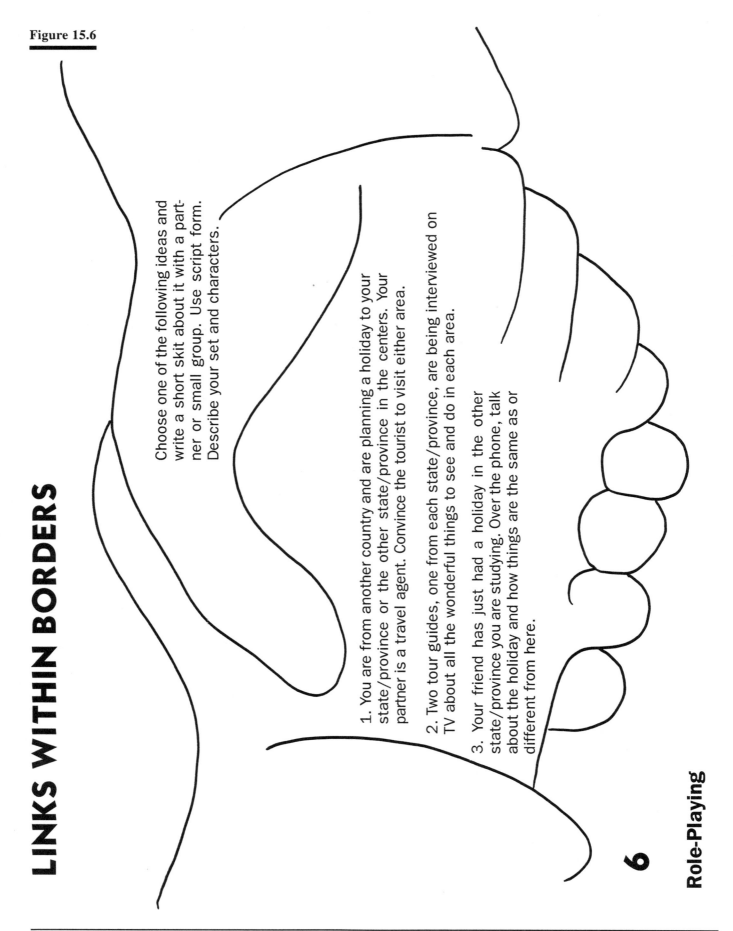

Choose one of the following ideas and write a short skit about it with a partner or small group. Use script form. Describe your set and characters.

1. You are from another country and are planning a holiday to your state/province or the other state/province in the centers. Your partner is a travel agent. Convince the tourist to visit either area.

2. Two tour guides, one from each state/province, are being interviewed on TV about all the wonderful things to see and do in each area.

3. Your friend has just had a holiday in the other state/province you are studying. Over the phone, talk about the holiday and how things are the same as or different from here.

6

Role-Playing

From *Library Centers.* © 1997 Judith A. Sykes. Libraries Unlimited. (800) 237-6124.

Figure 15.7

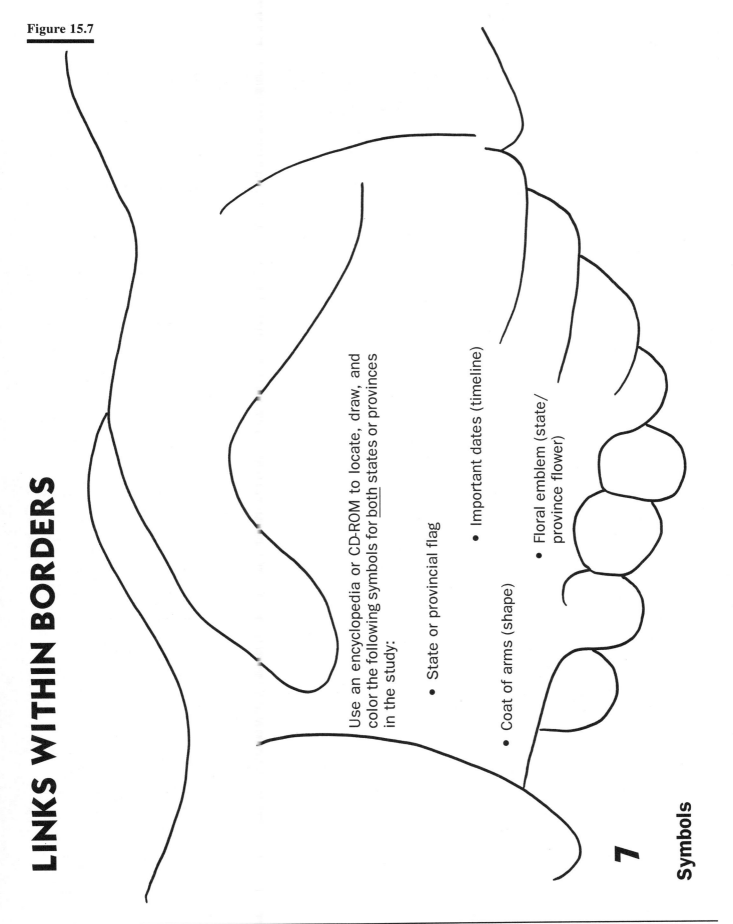

From *Library Centers* © 1997 Judith A. Sykes. Libraries Unlimited. (800) 237-6124.

Figure 15.8

LINKS WITHIN BORDERS
Checklist

Student Name: _____

Circle the number on this page when you have finished a center. Remember to comment about what you have learned and how you worked. Your teacher(s) will also comment.

1. Poster Maps.
    My comments: _____

    _____

    Teacher: _____

2. Sports Time.
    My comments: _____

    _____

    Teacher: _____

3. Tourism.
    My comments: _____

    _____

    Teacher: _____

4. Food Industry.
    My comments: _____

    _____

    Teacher: _____

5. Language/Culture.
    My comments: _____

    _____

    Teacher: _____

6. Role-Playing.
    My comments: _____

    _____

    Teacher: _____

7. Symbols.
    My comments: _____

    _____

    Teacher: _____

188   From *Library Centers*. © 1997 Judith A. Sykes. Libraries Unlimited. (800) 237-6124.

REGIONS

Chapter Sixteen

In these centers, students research a country's geographical regions and present an oral report about one particular region. Students are assigned to a specific region, such as mountains, plains, or desert. Students collect data at each of the centers using a chart such as the one shown in figure 16.1, page 190. After completing the centers, they must arrange good copies of collected data or projects to create a poster about their region.

Poster skills are taught in conjunction with these centers, giving students ideas for layout, cutting, adding dimension, lettering, and so on. Posters can be presented orally, with students highlighting an important part of their research or an interesting discovery. If your school has multimedia software such as "HyperStudio" available, the project takes the form of a hypermedia report. Suggestions for multimedia use are included under the "Method" headings of these centers.

The checklist at the end of this chapter (fig. 16.8, p. 200) can assist students with organization, self-assessment, and feedback. It can be used for an interim student report or sent home with the report card.

Viewing a center

Figure 16.1

REGIONS
Chart for Notes

Student name: _____

Name of region: _____

I CHARACTERISTICS LAND	II LOCATION	III CLIMATE	IV NATURAL RESOURCES/ INDUSTRIES

190   From *Library Centers*. © 1997 Judith A. Sykes. Libraries Unlimited. (800) 237-6124.

REGIONS 1

Materials Needed

- Regions 1 direction cards. (See fig. 16.2, p. 192.)
- Encyclopedias, CD-ROMs.
- White paper cut into 4" x 5" squares.

Method

Students will need assistance in understanding the difference between physical and political maps and how a region can overlap several states or provinces. Once they have discovered the states or provinces found within their region, they can use encyclopedias to look for their symbols. Drawings could be done on small white squares.

If you are using a hypermedia computer program, symbols can be downloaded from CD-ROMs or the Internet or scanned from print sources. Students can choose where they will place the graphics in their computer presentations.

REGIONS 2

Materials Needed

- Regions 2 direction cards. (See fig. 16.3, p. 193.)
- Visual material based on the regions of your country, from your collection or borrowed. Educational television companies may also be of service in providing materials.
- Audiovisuals from the Internet and CD-ROMs (such as "Encarta").

Method

During this center, students will learn how to set up a filmstrip, video, CD-ROM, or whatever medium you are using. Learning to take notes from an audiovisual medium can be challenging. They must listen for key words or ideas and learn that the topics on their chart will not be presented in order; hence, they may need to view the material more than once. Students should work together at this center, assisting each other in discussion: "Did you hear that? Was it important?"

They will also learn that not all of the information they require can be found in a particular source or sources. Sources available may be political (geared to the state or province) rather than regional; thus, students may have to view several short clips or filmstrips about states or provinces within their region to gather needed data.

An ideal resource that is becoming more readily available is laser disc. Students can literally "freeze-frame" key concepts, stop the video, and make their notes or download notes into a computer. If students are doing a hypermedia computer presentation, they can again download or scan materials pertaining to the chart topics.

191

Figure 16.2

REGIONS

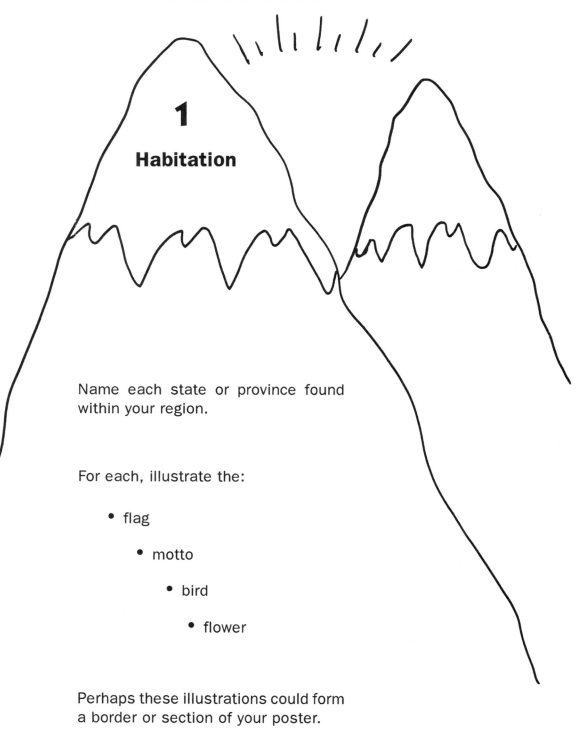

1 Habitation

Name each state or province found within your region.

For each, illustrate the:

- flag
- motto
- bird
- flower

Perhaps these illustrations could form a border or section of your poster.

From *Library Centers*. © 1997 Judith A. Sykes. Libraries Unlimited. (800) 237-6124.

Figure 16.3

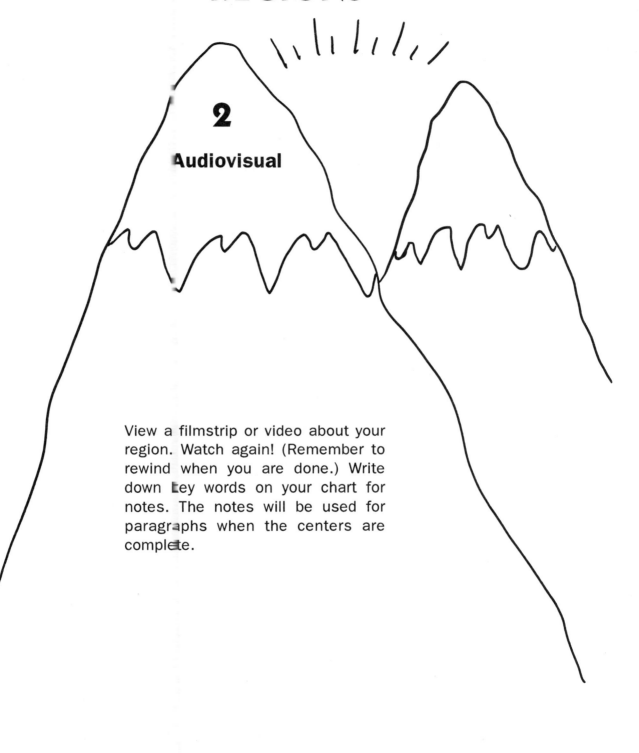

From *Library Centers.* © 1997 Judith A. Sykes. Libraries Unlimited. (800) 237-6124.

REGIONS 3

Materials Needed

- Regions 3 direction cards. (See fig. 16.4, p. 195.)
- Books on your country, especially large "coffee-table" books with colorful photographs.
- Pictures and vertical file material on the regions.
- 5.5" x 8.5" white paper (or 8.5" x 11" cut in half) for sketching.
- Colored construction paper cut slightly larger than the white sketch paper, for sketch "frames."

Method

Students may need assistance in finding pictures or information about their region within the books. They need to be encouraged to skim and browse to find parts of chapters that give them the data they need to add to their charts.

If students are doing a hypermedia computer presentation, they may wish to scan or type information onto cards from the books. Most multimedia software programs allow students to draw, so they may attempt their sketches this way if the equipment is available.

REGIONS 4

Materials Needed

- Regions 4 direction cards. (See fig. 16.5, p. 196.)
- Access to reference section.

Method

Students may need assistance with locating their regions in particular reference sources. The readability of encyclopedias and reference books varies, so students must practice scanning for the key words or concepts for their chart. Although they used encyclopedias at the first center for symbols, they are now reading deeper for written content. If students feel they have enough data after the first hour, they may wish to begin composing rough drafts of paragraphs.

If students are using a hypermedia computer approach, they could scan materials onto the computer for later editing and rewriting. Unless you have access to a number of computers, though, it might be better to have this group work with reference books and transfer the notes to a hypermedia stack when working on their presentations.

Figure 16.4

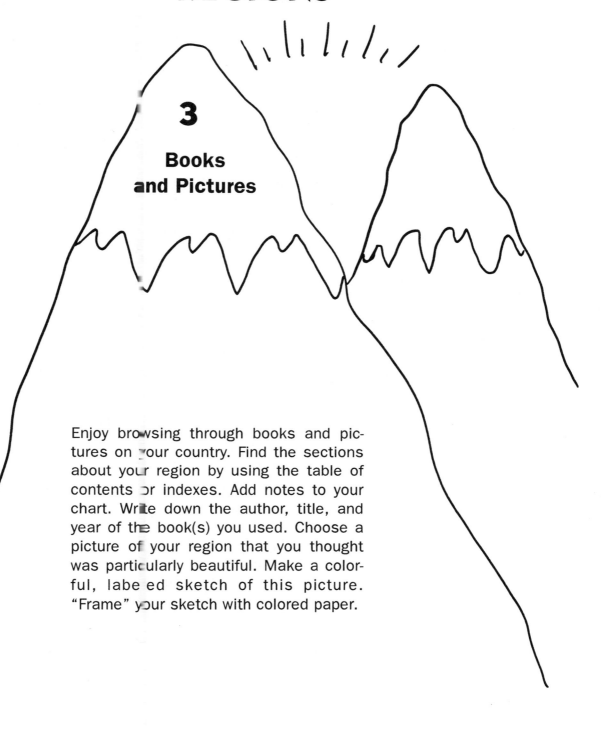

REGIONS

3

Books and Pictures

Enjoy browsing through books and pictures on your country. Find the sections about your region by using the table of contents or indexes. Add notes to your chart. Write down the author, title, and year of the book(s) you used. Choose a picture of your region that you thought was particularly beautiful. Make a colorful, labeled sketch of this picture. "Frame" your sketch with colored paper.

Figure 16.5

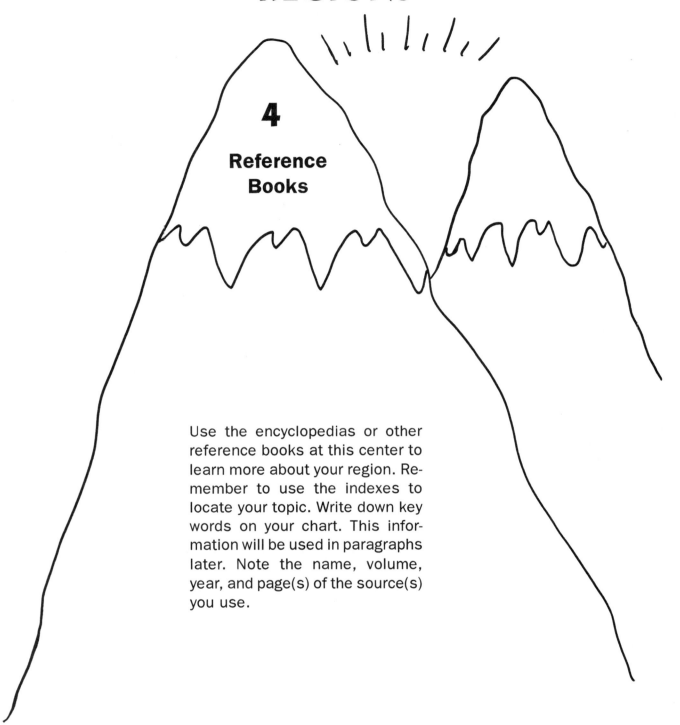

REGIONS

4

Reference Books

Use the encyclopedias or other reference books at this center to learn more about your region. Remember to use the indexes to locate your topic. Write down key words on your chart. This information will be used in paragraphs later. Note the name, volume, year, and page(s) of the source(s) you use.

From *Library Centers*. © 1997 Judith A. Sykes. Libraries Unlimited. (800) 237-6124.

REGIONS 5

Materials Needed

- Regions 5 direction cards. (See fig. 16.6, p. 198.)
- Books or reference sources of animals and plants common in your regions; access to the catalog to retrieve materials on specific plants and animals.
- 4" x 5" drawing paper or discarded nature magazines for cutting up.

Method

Students may come to the center already knowledgeable about flora and fauna of their area, or they may need to discover these things about their subject region. Students who already have a general knowledge base may opt to use the catalog to find books on specific plants or animals. They will need encouragement in their sketching and searching.

REGIONS 6

Materials Needed

- Regions 6 direction cards. (See fig. 16.7, p. 199.)
- Variety of atlases of the country.
- Construction paper, stencils for letters, scissors.
- Blank maps of your country.

Method

Students may require assistance in finding physical maps of their regions to sketch and also in finding map symbols or legends pertaining to natural resources or industry.

If students are doing hypermedia reports, they can create their titles using fonts and sounds in the computer program. They can scan their maps and illustrations into the computer later. Students using the hypermedia computer approach could still be encouraged to do their own drawings or cutouts and then scan them when time permits.

197

Figure 16.6

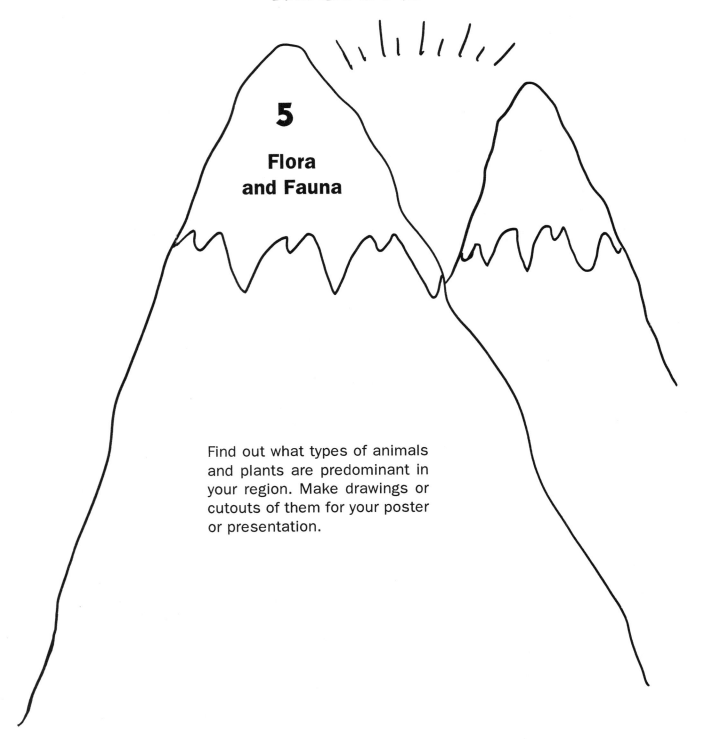

198 From *Library Centers*. © 1997 Judith A. Sykes. Libraries Unlimited. (800) 237-6124.

Figure 16.7

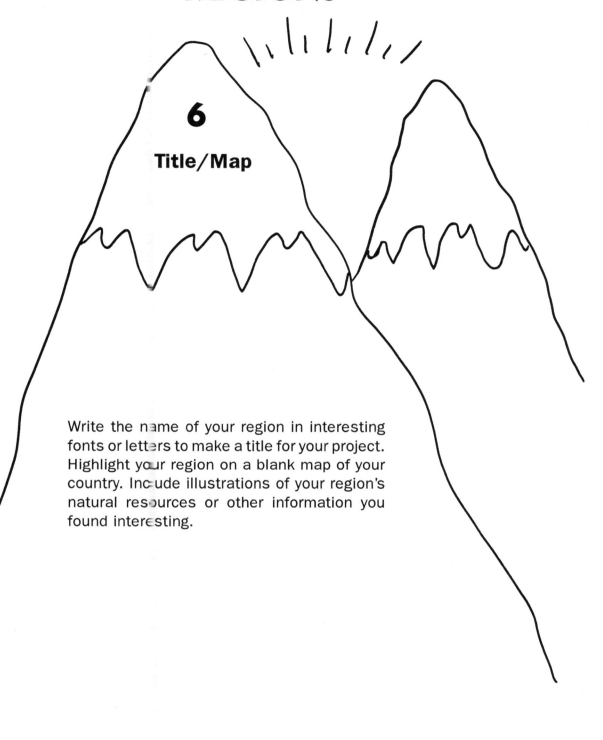

REGIONS

6

Title/Map

Write the name of your region in interesting fonts or letters to make a title for your project. Highlight your region on a blank map of your country. Include illustrations of your region's natural resources or other information you found interesting.

From *Library Centers*. © 1997 Judith A. Sykes. Libraries Unlimited. (800) 237-6124.

Figure 16.8

REGIONS
Checklist

Student Name: _____

CENTER	STUDENT COMMENTS	TEACHER COMMENTS
1. Habitation		
__ Four symbols per state/ province		
2. Audiovisual		
__ Regional key words		
3. Books and Pictures		
__ Key words		
__ Sketch		
4. Reference Books		
__ Key words		
__ Bibliography		
__ Paragraphs		
5. Flora and Fauna		
__ Three visuals		
6. Title/Map		
__ Lettering		
__ Region highlighted		
__ Illustrations		
Poster or Multimedia Presentation		

200 From *Library Centers*. © 1997 Judith A. Sykes. Libraries Unlimited. (800) 237-6124.

EXPLORATION

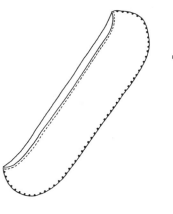

Chapter Seventeen

The following centers enhance a study of a country's early explorers, from about the 1600s through the 1800s. In these centers, students use resources to learn more about these intrepid adventurers and their times. They will be investigating underlying issues of survival, native encounters and cultures, trading, early settlements, and discovery.

The checklist at the end of this chapter (fig. 17.7, p. 211) can assist students with organization, self-assessment, and feedback. It can be used for an interim student report or sent home with the report card.

EXPLORATION 1

Materials Needed

- Exploration 1 direction cards. (See fig. 17.1, p. 202.)
- Books, encyclopedias, and other materials in your collection that best detail early native culture.
- Blank overhead transparencies.
- Thin felt-tip markers for overhead transparencies.

Method

Students may need assistance in locating and listing names of native cultures prevalent in their country during the seventeenth century. Once they locate a tribe and choose a heading, the information required will usually be quite accessible in the source under that heading. Each student contributes to the group presentation with his or her own overhead on one of the topic headings. Students will need to practice with the overhead projector before making their presentations.

201

Figure 17.1

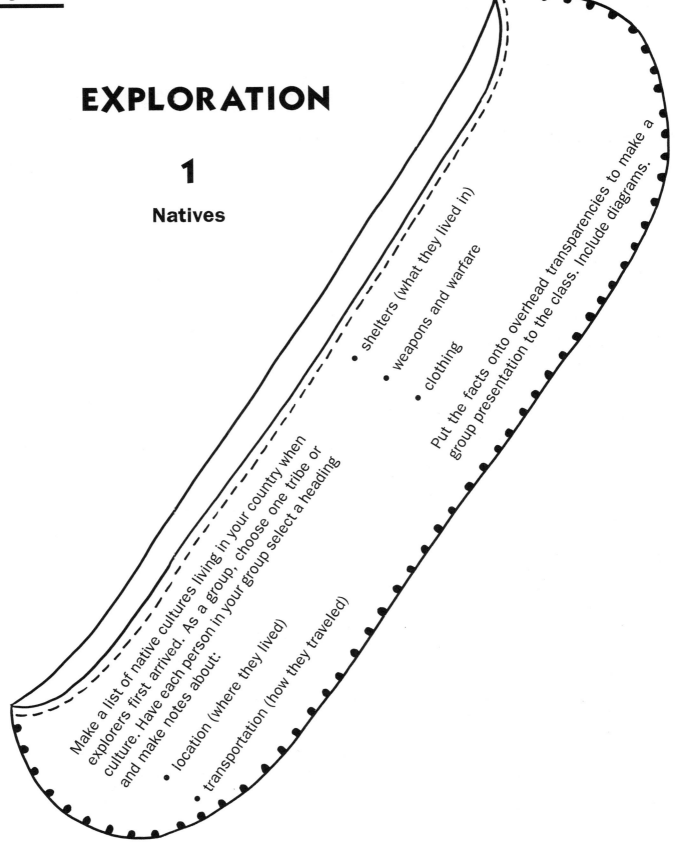

From *Library Centers*. © 1997 Judith A. Sykes. Libraries Unlimited. (800) 237-6124.

EXPLORATION 2

Materials Needed

- Exploration 2 direction cards. (See fig. 17.2, p. 204.)
- Copies of January 1986 *National Geographic* or other information on the Franklin Expedition. An interesting novel study for this topic is Martyn Godfrey's *Mystery of the Frozen Lands.*
- Half-size cream-colored poster paper (10" x 12").
- Stencils or computer fonts for "antique" title.
- Pens, felt-tip markers.

Method

Students find the Franklin Expedition fascinating, despite its tragic ending. Students may need to discuss why Franklin's final expedition failed. Instead of Franklin, you may wish to highlight another explorer, perhaps a notable figure in your area or curriculum or a person on whom you have other resources or *National Geographic* articles. Students may need assistance in designing posters.

EXPLORATION 3

Materials Needed

- Exploration 3 direction cards. (See fig. 17.3, p. 205.)
- Encyclopedia/CD-ROM access.
- Large roll of mural paper.

Method

Students may need assistance in choosing a battle and locating the required information. You may wish to specify a famous battle from your area's history (for example, the battle of the Plains of Abraham, Generals Wolfe and Montcalm). Have some students create the title for the mural. The mural is added to as each group gets to the center. You may want to put it on a large table or the floor. Written work will require editing before it is transferred onto the mural. Illustrations could include sketches of the generals' portraits, battle strategy, uniforms, weapons, peace treaties, and so on.

Figure 17.2

EXPLORATION

2

Franklin Expedition

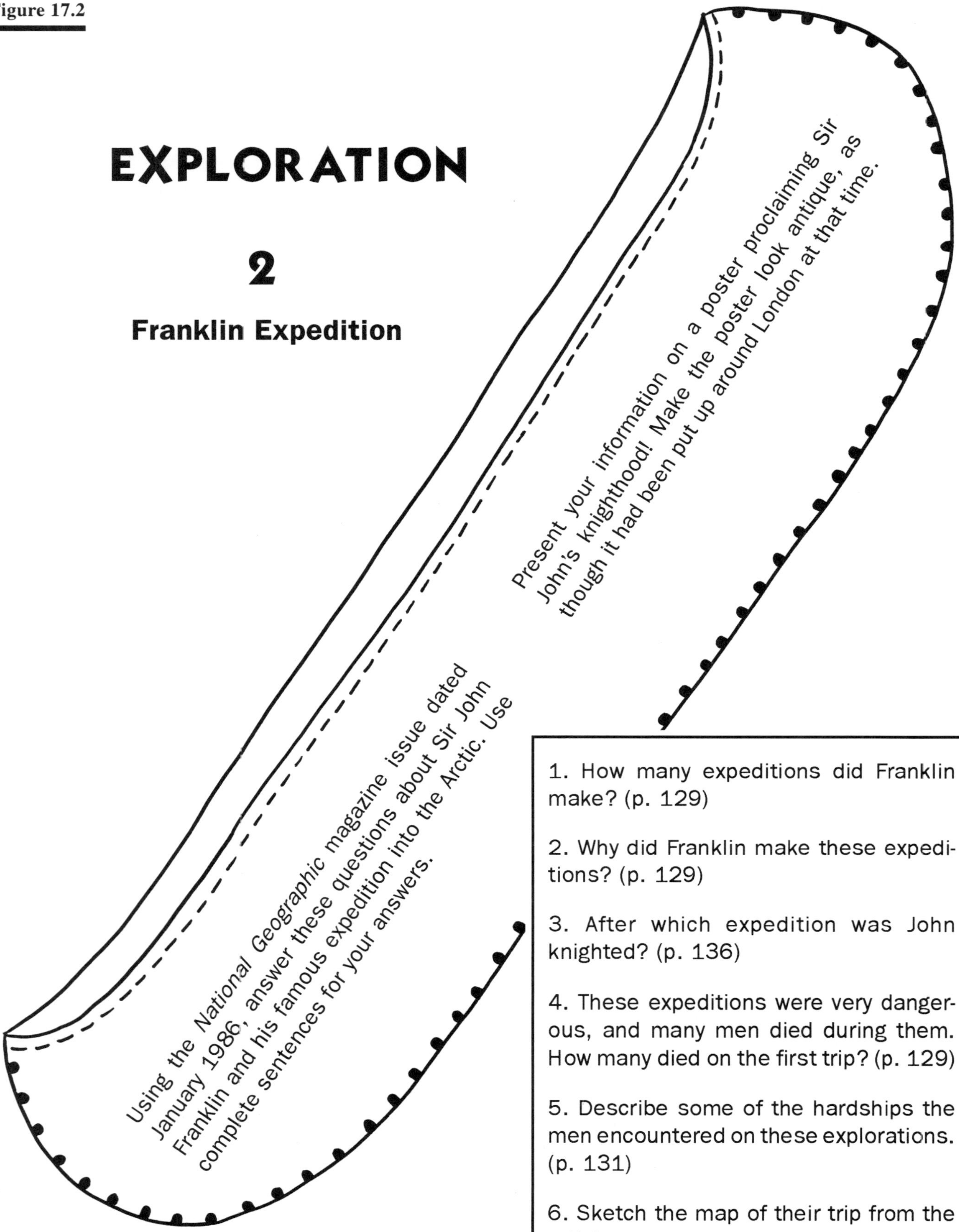

Present your information on a poster proclaiming Sir John's knighthood! Make the poster look antique, as though it had been put up around London at that time.

Using the *National Geographic* magazine issue dated January 1986, answer these questions about Sir John Franklin and his famous expedition into the Arctic. Use complete sentences for your answers.

1. How many expeditions did Franklin make? (p. 129)

2. Why did Franklin make these expeditions? (p. 129)

3. After which expedition was John knighted? (p. 136)

4. These expeditions were very dangerous, and many men died during them. How many died on the first trip? (p. 129)

5. Describe some of the hardships the men encountered on these explorations. (p. 131)

6. Sketch the map of their trip from the article.

204   From *Library Centers*. © 1997 Judith A. Sykes. Libraries Unlimited. (800) 237-6124.

Figure 17.3

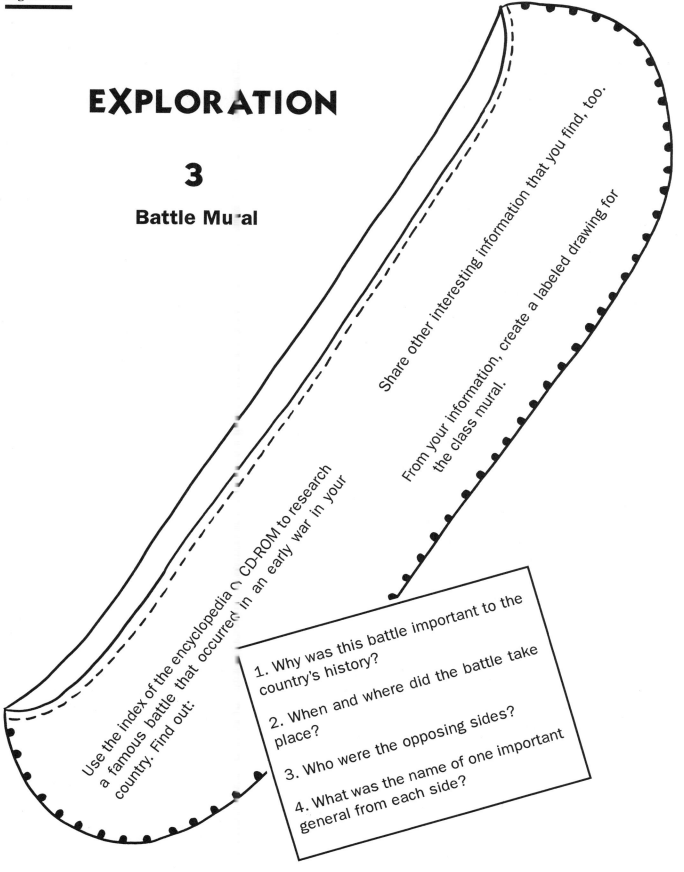

EXPLORATION 3
Battle Mural

Use the index of the encyclopedia CD-ROM to research a famous battle that occurred in an early war in your country. Find out:

1. Why was this battle important to the country's history?
2. When and where did the battle take place?
3. Who were the opposing sides?
4. What was the name of one important general from each side?

Share other interesting information that you find, too.

From your information, create a labeled drawing for the class mural.

From *Library Centers*. © 1997 Judith A. Sykes. Libraries Unlimited. (800) 237-6124. 205

EXPLORATION 4

Materials Needed

- Exploration 4 direction cards. (See fig. 17.4, p. 207.)
- Encyclopedias, CD-ROMs, historical reference materials.
- Blank maps of your country.
- Atlases, historical atlases.
- Pens and paper for writing.

Method

Students may need assistance locating and choosing early explorers. You may want to include a center card that specifies names from your curriculum (for example, Columbus, Cabot, Hudson). After students discover what parts of the country the explorer explored, they may need help in marking their maps with this information. Historical atlases often show the routes and may make it easier for some students to follow.

EXPLORATION 5

Materials Needed

- Exploration 5 direction cards. (See fig. 17.5, p. 208.)
- Books, pictures, and other library materials on early settlements in your country.
- White paper or art paper for the diaries.

Method

Students may occasionally need you to join in the discussion and findings as they research. They may not discover all "answers" to the guiding questions, but they will certainly find other interesting information for their diaries. Encourage students to imagine that they are early settlers, writing as they would have back then. The diaries will require editing.

Figure 17.4

EXPLORATION

4

Explorer Routes

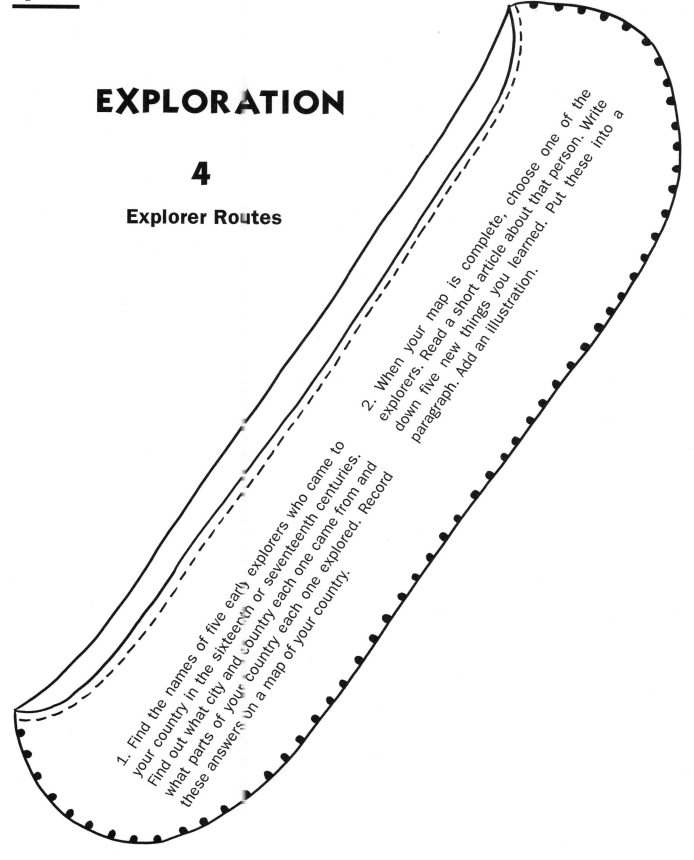

1. Find the names of five early explorers who came to your country in the sixteenth or seventeenth centuries. Find out what city and country each one came from and what parts of your country each one explored. Record these answers on a map of your country.

2. When your map is complete, choose one of the explorers. Read a short article about that person. Write down five new things you learned. Put these into a paragraph. Add an illustration.

From *Library Centers.* © 1997 Judith A. Sykes. Libraries Unlimited. (800) 237-6124.   207

Figure 17.5

EXPLORATION

5

Early Settlement

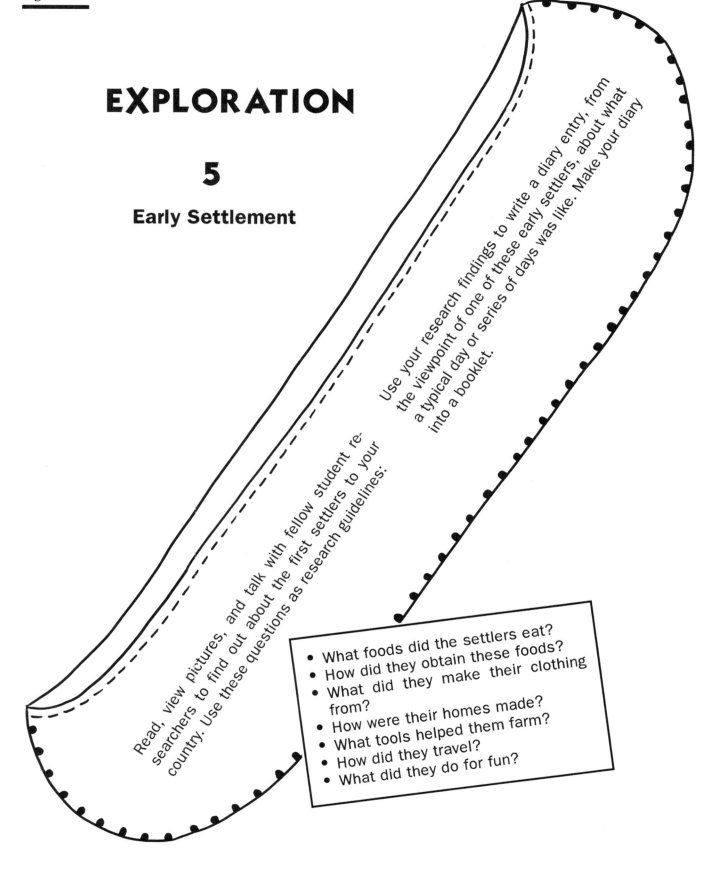

Read, view pictures, and talk with fellow student researchers to find out about the first settlers to your country. Use these questions as research guidelines:

Use your research findings to write a diary entry, from the viewpoint of one of these early settlers, about what a typical day or series of days was like. Make your diary into a booklet.

- What foods did the settlers eat?
- How did they obtain these foods?
- What did they make their clothing from?
- How were their homes made?
- What tools helped them farm?
- How did they travel?
- What did they do for fun?

From *Library Centers*. © 1997 Judith A. Sykes. Libraries Unlimited. (800) 237-6124.

EXPLORATION 6

Materials Needed

- Exploration 6 direct on cards. (See fig. 17.6, p. 210.)
- Books or other reference materials on the topic.
- Examples of early poetry, if available; some explorers, such as Henry Kelsey, wrote poetry.

Method

This center may include group discussion or readings. Students need to know that their poems are to be based on images and feelings inspired by their key words and need not necessarily rhyme or follow a particular poetic form. If word processors are available, students may wish to compose on the computer.

Figure 17.6

EXPLORATION

6

Interaction

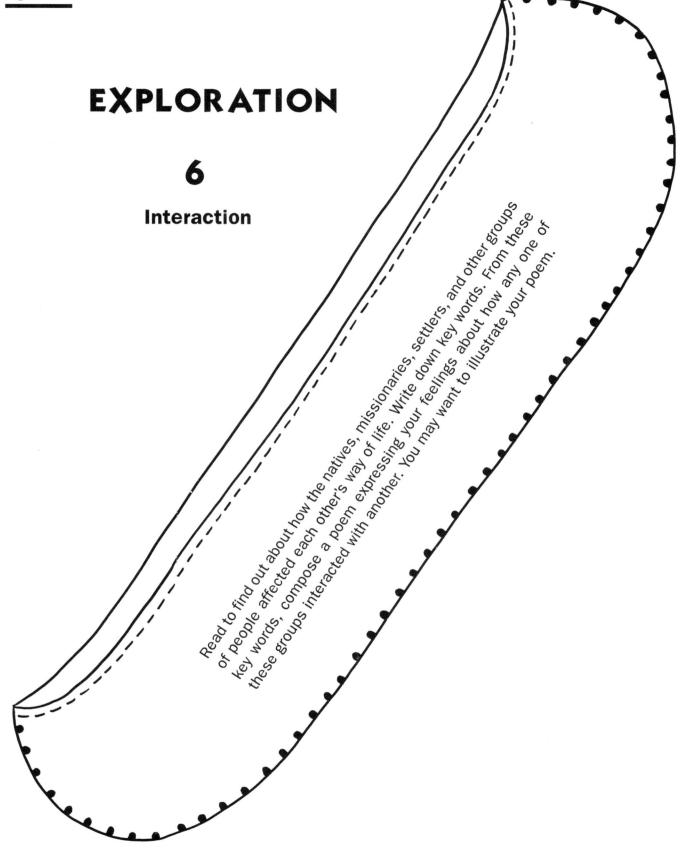

Read to find out about how the natives, missionaries, settlers, and other groups of people affected each other's way of life. Write down key words. From these key words, compose a poem expressing your feelings about how any one of these groups interacted with another. You may want to illustrate your poem.

210 From Library Centers. *© 1997 Judith A. Sykes. Libraries Unlimited. (800) 237-6124.*

Figure 17.7

EXPLORATION
Checklist

Student Name: _____

CENTER	STUDENT COMMENTS	TEACHER COMMENTS
1. Natives		
__ Transparencies		
__ Presentation		
2. Franklin Expedition [or another explorer]		
__ Poster		
3. Battle Mural		
__ Mural contribution		
4. Explorer Routes		
__ Map		
__ Paragraph		
5. Early Settlement		
__ Diary		
6. Interaction		
__ Poem		

From *Library Centers*. © 1997 Judith A. Sykes. Libraries Unlimited. (800) 237-6124.

LINKS ACROSS BORDERS

Chapter Eighteen

The purpose of these centers is to celebrate the multi-ethnic origins of countries. You may wish to specify certain countries that are or were predominant in your own country's history, or you may choose a multicultural approach. You could organize a celebration that includes center displays, presentations, and ethnic foods.

The checklist at the end of this chapter (fig. 18.7, p. 222) can assist students with organization, self-assessment, and feedback. It can be used for an interim student report or sent home with the report card.

LINKS ACROSS BORDERS 1

Materials Needed

- Links Across Borders 1 direction cards. (See fig. 18.1, p. 214.)
- General reference books, such as encyclopedias and CD-ROMs, Web sites.
- Specific books on countries you have chosen to highlight.
- 10" x 12" art paper.

Method

Some discussion may be necessary to start students thinking about the different foods, sports, clothing, or other things that have come to your country from other cultures. Students may need encouragement on their drawings or design.

213

Figure 18.1

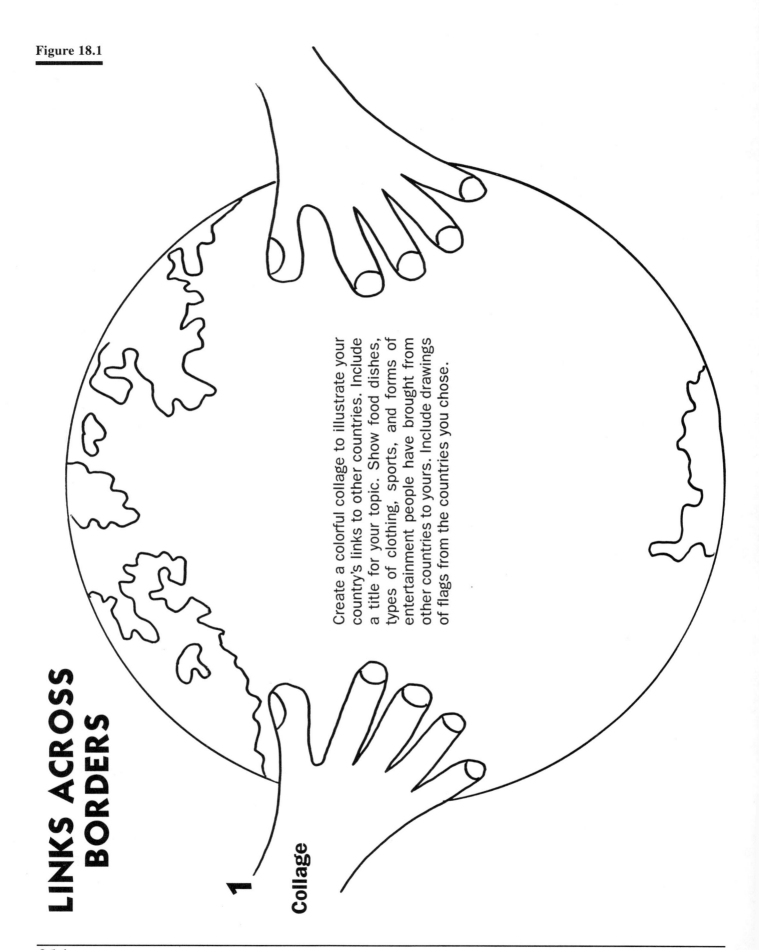

LINKS ACROSS BORDERS 2

Materials Needed

- Links Across Borders 2 direction cards. (See fig. 18.2, p. 216.)
- Donated newspapers from at least the last two weeks (replace these as they become too cut-up).

Method

The challenge in this center is not only finding articles about your country and another but also having students read them for understanding. Does the article really provide information about how the countries are linked? How can the students explain this in their own words? Their work will require editing and discussion.

LINKS ACROSS BORDERS 3

Materials Needed

- Links Across Borders 3 direction cards. (See fig. 18.3, p. 217.)
- Cookbooks.
- Blank world maps.
- Atlases or globes.
- Pencils, felt-tip pens

Method

Students may need assistance while using tables of contents or indexes of cookbooks to find recipes from other countries. They may need help in finding the countries in an atlas or on a globe. Students may wish to list or bring recipes from countries of their own ethnic background.

Figure 18.2

LINKS ACROSS BORDERS

2 Current Affairs

Using newspapers, find at least two articles that show links between your country and another. Cut out and paste the articles on lined paper. Under each article, explain in complete sentences how your country is linked with the country in the article.

From *Library Centers*. © 1997 Judith A. Sykes. Libraries Unlimited. (800) 237-6124.

Figure 18.3

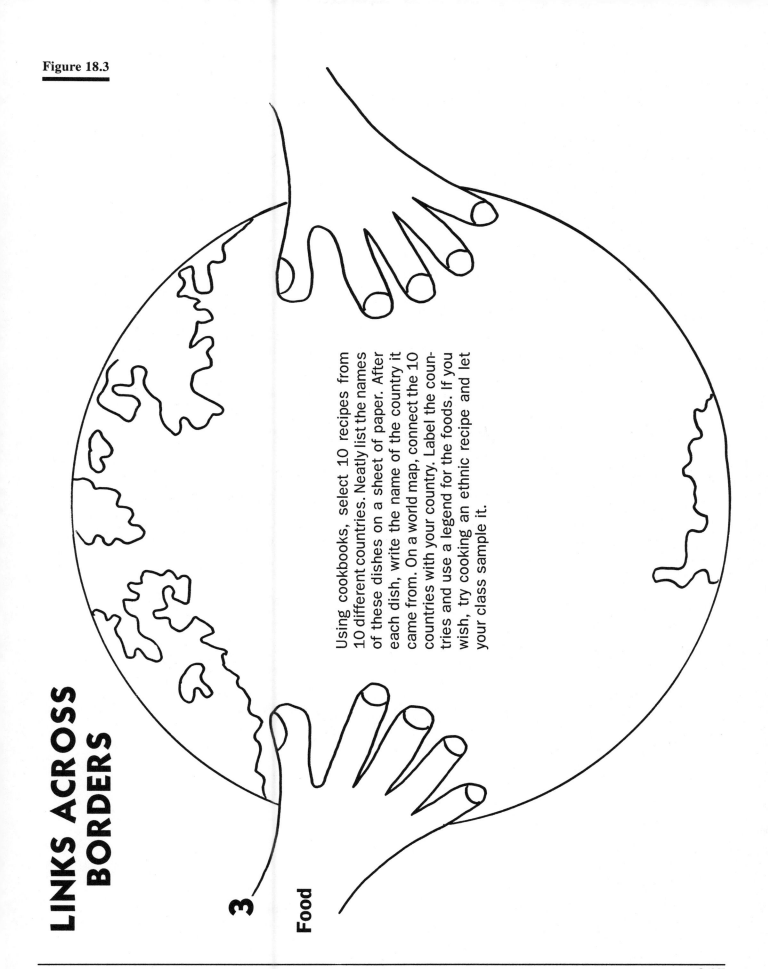

LINKS ACROSS BORDERS

3

Food

Using cookbooks, select 10 recipes from 10 different countries. Neatly list the names of these dishes on a sheet of paper. After each dish, write the name of the country it came from. On a world map, connect the 10 countries with your country. Label the countries and use a legend for the foods. If you wish, try cooking an ethnic recipe and let your class sample it.

From *Library Centers*. © 1997 Judith A. Sykes. Libraries Unlimited. (800) 237-6124.

LINKS ACROSS BORDERS 4

Materials Needed

- Links Across Borders 4 direction cards. (See fig. 18.4, p. 219.)
- Picture books or collections of short stories (e.g., fairy tales or legends) from other lands.
- Videotapes and video camera (or audiotape and tape recorder, if video is not available).

Method

Students may read as a group or in pairs. Books from the junior fairy tale section of the library will demonstrate to students that there are many diverse tales from different lands. Some students may need assistance with bibliographic form (author's name with last name first, title, publisher, year, and annotation). Most will need practice with storytelling for the video or oral presentation. The videotapes can be enjoyed by younger grades.

LINKS ACROSS BORDERS 5

Materials Needed

- Links Across Borders 5 direction cards. (See fig. 18.5, p. 220.)
- General encyclopedias, CD-ROMs, and specialized sources, such as the Lands and Peoples encyclopedia or the "National Geographic Picture Atlas of the World" CD-ROM.

Method

Students may need assistance in locating topics in the reference books and in writing down pertinent key words or phrases. Their writing will have to be edited.

LINKS ACROSS BORDERS 6

Materials Needed

- Links Across Borders 6 direction cards. (See fig. 18.6, p. 221.)
- Access to periodicals.
- Access to collection.
- Shelf markers.

Method

Students may need assistance in finding the place of publication within the various materials. They may also need guidance in composing an opinion paragraph from their research results.

218

Figure 18.4

LINKS ACROSS BORDERS

4

Literature Links

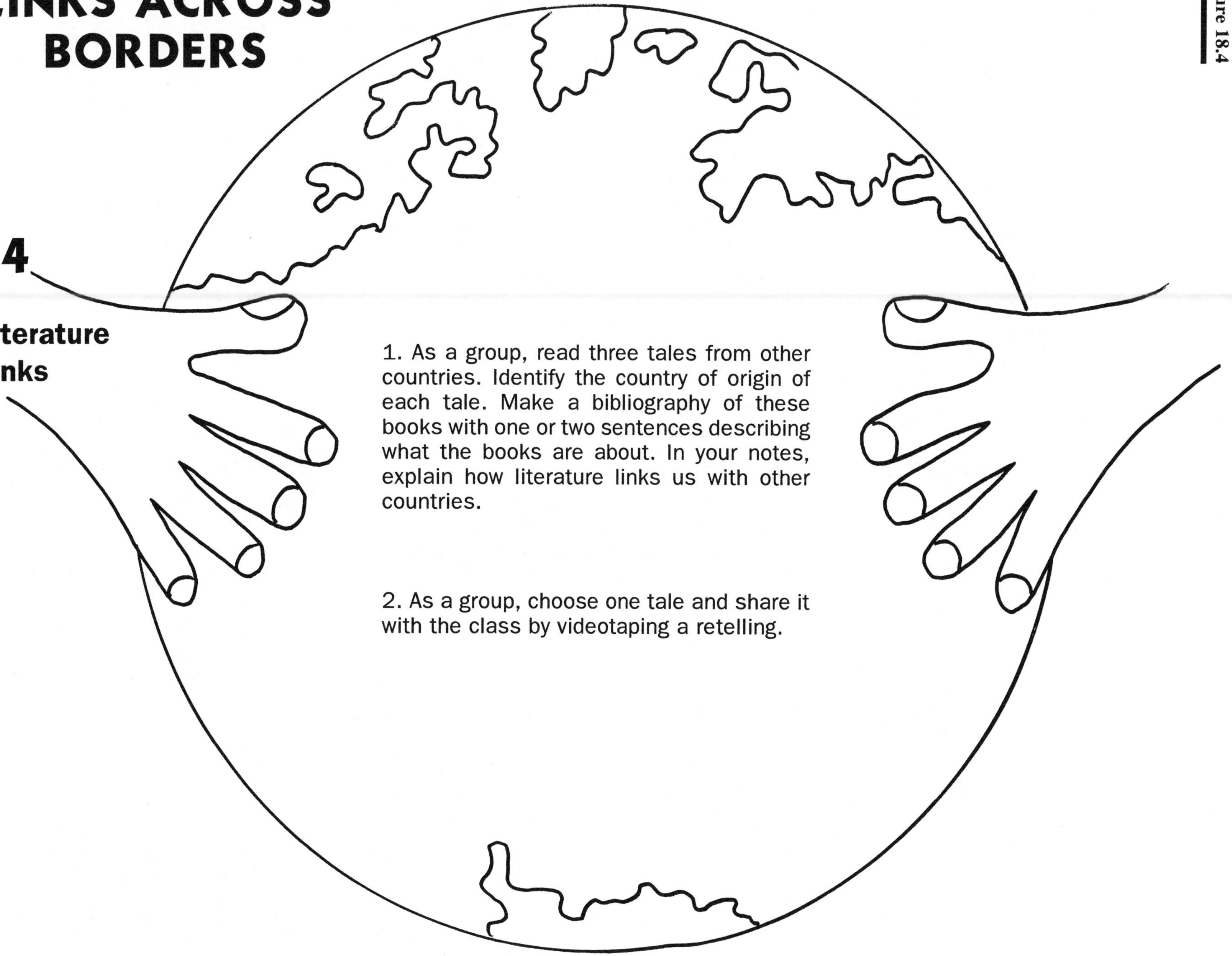

1. As a group, read three tales from other countries. Identify the country of origin of each tale. Make a bibliography of these books with one or two sentences describing what the books are about. In your notes, explain how literature links us with other countries.

2. As a group, choose one tale and share it with the class by videotaping a retelling.

From *Library Centers*. © 1997 Judith A. Sykes. Libraries Unlimited. (800) 237-6124.

Figure 18.5

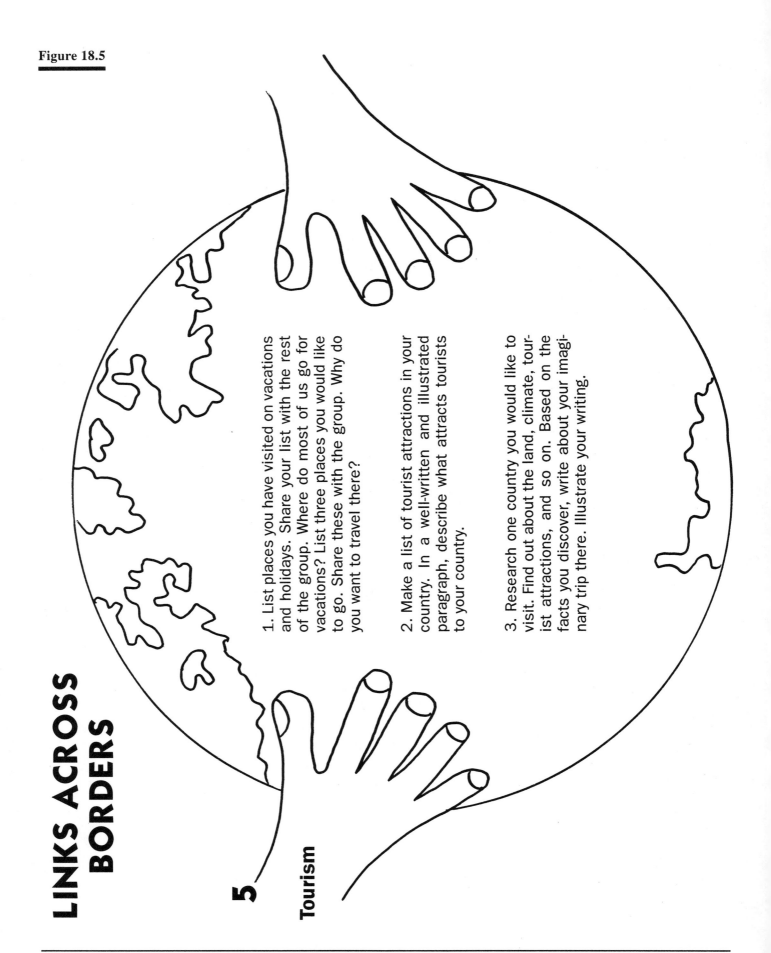

LINKS ACROSS BORDERS

5

Tourism

1. List places you have visited on vacations and holidays. Share your list with the rest of the group. Where do most of us go for vacations? List three places you would like to go. Share these with the group. Why do you want to travel there?

2. Make a list of tourist attractions in your country. In a well-written and illustrated paragraph, describe what attracts tourists to your country.

3. Research one country you would like to visit. Find out about the land, climate, tourist attractions, and so on. Based on the facts you discover, write about your imaginary trip there. Illustrate your writing.

220 From *Library Centers*. © 1997 Judith A. Sykes. Libraries Unlimited. (800) 237-6124.

Figure 18.6

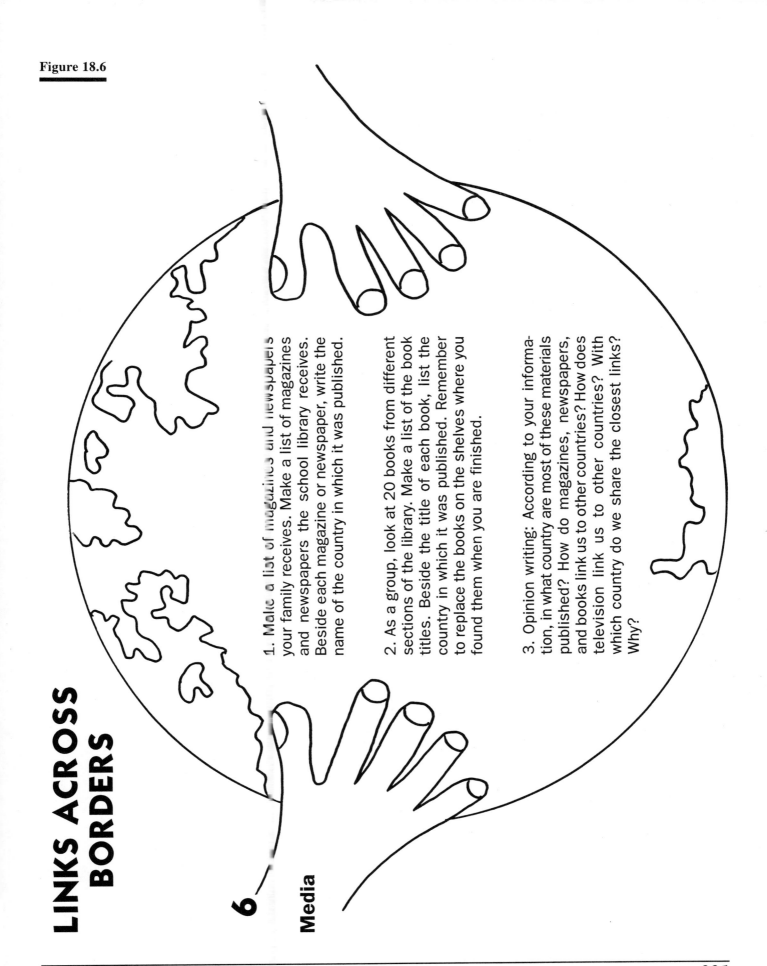

LINKS ACROSS BORDERS

6.

Media

1. Make a list of magazines and newspapers your family receives. Make a list of magazines and newspapers the school library receives. Beside each magazine or newspaper, write the name of the country in which it was published.

2. As a group, look at 20 books from different sections of the library. Make a list of the book titles. Beside the title of each book, list the country in which it was published. Remember to replace the books on the shelves where you found them when you are finished.

3. Opinion writing: According to your information, in what country are most of these materials published? How do magazines, newspapers, and books link us to other countries? How does television link us to other countries? With which country do we share the closest links? Why?

From *Library Centers* © 1997 Judith A. Sykes. Libraries Unlimited. (800) 237-6124.

Figure 18.7

LINKS ACROSS BORDERS
Checklist

Student Name: _____

CENTER	STUDENT COMMENTS	TEACHER COMMENTS
1. Collage		
__ Collage complete		
2. Current Affairs		
__ Two articles with summary comments		
3. Food		
__ List		
__ Map		
4. Literature Links		
__ Bibliography		
__ Retelling (videotape)		
5. Tourism		
__ List(s)		
__ Paragraph		
__ Story		
6. Media		
__ Research results		
__ Opinion writing		

222   From *Library Centers*. © 1997 Judith A. Sykes. Libraries Unlimited. (800) 237-6124.

CENTER TIPS

Chapter Nineteen

Getting started

As you become familiar with using library centers, you will come up with observations of your own. The following suggestions may assist you in learning the process or in implementation.

- Start center time by bringing students together for questions and instructions at the first session. When necessary, gather them for shorter question or instruction periods in later sessions.

- Hand out portfolios, scribblers, and other materials students will need along with checklists.

- You may want to designate a student or students from each group to take turns bringing the resources to the center location and returning them to a designated location at the end of the session.

- Centers could stay in one spot, with groups moving when it is time to change centers.

- Materials should be located near the resources needed, such as the reference area, video area, art area, and so on.

- Students should keep areas organized; before students leave, chairs should be pushed in and materials should be returned to bins or boxes.

- Center cards may be read and completed by individuals reading silently or one person reading to the group.

- Students should record the name and number of each center. When students finish a center that has an evaluation checklist, they should write about the center in the student comment space and then have the teacher or teacher-librarian sign the checklist.

- Themes can be adapted to any grade level. Both first-grade and fifth-grade students enjoyed researching "whales" and "Egypt" in a center approach.

- Create centers with whatever materials you have or can easily borrow. For instance, you may have a filmstrip or a book or an encyclopedia on Egyptian mummies.

- If some center themes catch on and are used in other years, or are curriculum requirements, consider them in relation to collection development. For example, you may hear about a great new video or CD-ROM on your topic. Also, any topic can be explored in an Internet center.

- Centers may lead to additional enrichment or discoveries by your students. Let them take the lead in expanding and changing centers.

- Have teachers and students evaluate centers on an ongoing basis.

- Make sure that some centers have more independent activities than others, so that if only the teacher-librarian or teacher are circulating, students at those centers can continue their work.

- Make sure that center activities call on a mix of learning styles, using the multisensory approach.

Boris Ramirez

Arroces : cocina para todos / ilustraciones José Luis Hernanz Hernández ;
  fotografía Fernando Ramajo. -- Santafé de Bogotá : Panamericana Editorial,
  1999.
  32 p. : il. ; 15 cm. -- (Cocina para todos ; 8)
  ISBN 958-30-0601-7
  2. Cocina 2. Arroz (Cocina) I. Hernanz Hernández, José Luis, il. II. Ramajo,
Fernando, il. III. Serie
641.6318 cd 20 ed.
AGQ0609

CEP-Biblioteca Luis-Angel Arango

Editor
Panamericana Editorial Ltda.

Dirección editorial
Alberto Ramírez Santos

Edición
Gabriel Silva Rincón

Realización editorial
Simpei, SL

Diseño
Itos Vazquez

Ilustraciones
José Luis Hernanz Hernández

Fotografía
Fernando Ramajo

Selección de recetas, cocina y estilismo
Itos Vazquez

Primera edición, Editorial Voluntad S.A., 1995
Cuarta edición en Panamericana Editorial Ltda., mayo de 2000

© 2000 Panamericana Editorial Ltda.
Calle 12 No. 34-20, Tels.: 3603077 - 2770100
Fax: (57 1) 2373805
Correo electrónico: panaedit@andinet.com
www.panamericanaeditorial.com.co
Santafé de Bogotá, D. C., Colombia

ISBN volumen: 958-30-0601-7
ISBN colección: 958-30-0599-1

Todos los derechos reservados.
Prohibida su reproducción total o parcial
por cualquier medio sin permiso del Editor.

Impreso por Panamericana Formas e Impresos S. A.
Calle 65 No. 94-72, Tels.: 4302110 - 4300355, Fax: (57 1) 2763008
Quien sólo actúa como impresor.

Impreso en Colombia   Printed in Colombia

ARROCES

COCINA PARA TODOS

Arroz con Embutidos

Ingredientes para 4 personas:

350 g de arroz de grano redondo
6 cucharadas de aceite de oliva
50 g de longaniza cortada en trocitos
50 g de chorizo picante cortado en trocitos
100 g de jamón serrano picado
2 dientes de ajo picados
1 cucharada de perejil picado
1 pimiento rojo seco, remojado
Caldo de gallina (el doble del volumen de arroz)
5 cucharadas de pasta de tomate
Sal

Calentar el aceite en una cazuela de barro y rehogar la longaniza, el chorizo y el jamón, revolviendo constantemente para que no se peguen.

A continuación, machacar en un mortero los ajos con el perejil, el pimiento y sal, e incorporar a la cazuela. Agregar el arroz, revolver bien, rociar con el caldo y la pasta de tomate, rectificar la sazón y cocinar hasta que el arroz esté en su punto.

Servir de inmediato.

Paella

Ingredientes para 6 personas:
750 g de arroz ~ 8 cucharadas de aceite
1/2 pollo despresado ~ 1/2 conejo despresado
1/2 lb de habichuelas frescas cortadas en trozos
2 alcachofas limpias y cortadas en cuartos ~ 1 cabeza entera de ajos
2 tomates muy maduros, pelados y picados ~ 2 1/2 litros de agua
3 dientes de ajo ~ 1 cucharada de perejil picado
1 cucharadita de color ~ 1 ramita de tomillo ~ 1 ramita de romero
150 g de fríjoles blancos tiernos (opcional) ~ Sal

Calentar el aceite en una paellera y dorar el pollo y el conejo. Añadir las habichuelas, las alcachofas y la cabeza de ajos y rehogar. Agregar los tomates, revolver y rociar con el agua.

Machacar los dientes de ajo y el perejil con sal y agregar a la paellera. Cocinar a fuego alto durante 15 minutos.

Mientras tanto, machacar en un mortero el color, el tomillo, y el romero. Incorporar a la paellera con los fríjoles, si se utilizan. Añadir el arroz, extender con una paleta y cocinar durante 10 minutos a fuego alto. Bajar el fuego y cocinar durante otros 10 minutos. Retirar del fuego, dejar reposar durante 10 minutos y servir.

Arroz a la Campesina

Ingredientes para 4 personas:
250 g de arroz de grano largo
7 cucharadas de aceite
1 cebolla picada
2 dientes de ajo finamente picados
1 calabacín mediano cortado en trocitos
100 g de arvejas
100 g de jamón cortado en tiritas
4 cucharadas de queso Emmental, rallado
2 cucharadas de pimiento rojo, picado
2 cucharadas de pasta de tomate
4 tazas de caldo de gallina (puede ser en cubitos)
Sal y pimienta blanca

Calentar el aceite en una olla y rehogar la cebolla y los ajos hasta que empiecen a dorarse.

A continuación, agregar el calabacín, las arvejas, el jamón, el queso, el pimiento y la pasta de tomate. Sazonar con sal y pimienta y sofreír durante 5 minutos.

Por último, añadir el arroz, revolver bien, rociar con el caldo y cocinar durante 20 minutos. Dejar reposar durante 5 minutos y servir.

Arroz Delicioso

Ingredientes para 4-6 personas:

2 tazas de arroz
1 vasito de aceite
2 dientes de ajo picados
1 pechuga de pollo cortada en trocitos
4 higaditos de pollo cortados en trocitos
1/2 lb de lomito de cerdo cortado en trocitos
100 g de jamón picado
100 g de chorizo cortado en rodajas ~ 100 g de arvejas
4 tazas de caldo de res caliente
2 pimientos rojos enlatados
2 huevos duros ~ Sal y pimienta

Calentar el aceite en una cazuela de barro y rehogar los ajos. Agregar la pechuga y los higaditos de pollo, el lomito, el jamón y el chorizo y freír durante unos minutos.

A continuación, añadir las arvejas y el arroz, revolver todo bien, rociar con el caldo caliente y sazonar con sal y pimienta.

Por último, cocinar a fuego bajo durante 25 minutos o hasta que el arroz esté suelto y seco. Decorar con los huevos y los pimientos, dejar reposar durante 5 minutos y servir.

Arroz a la Cubana

Ingredientes para 4 personas:
250 g de arroz
3 cucharadas de aceite
2 dientes de ajo picados
Agua (el doble del volumen de arroz)
4 plátanos pelados y cortados por la mitad en sentido longitudinal
1 cucharada de mantequilla
4 huevos ~ Aceite para freír
8 salchichas
1 lb de pasta de tomate ~ Sal

Calentar el aceite en una olla y dorar los ajos. Incorporar el arroz y revolver con una cuchara de madera hasta que absorba la grasa. Rociar con el agua, salar y cocinar hasta que el arroz esté en su punto y haya absorbido el agua.

Mientras tanto, freír los plátanos en la mantequilla, dándoles la vuelta para que estén bien dorados.

A continuación, freír los huevos y las salchichas; calentar la pasta de tomate.

Por último, presentar los platos poniendo en cada uno 1 huevo, 2 salchichas, 1 plátano y arroz blanco rociado con la pasta de tomate.

Arroz al Vino Tinto

Ingredientes para 4 personas:
300 g de arroz
4 cucharadas de aceite
1/2 cebolla picada
Unas hojitas de romero
1 cucharada de tomate picado
300 g de carne molida de res
150 ml de vino tinto
Caldo de gallina
Sal y pimienta

Calentar el aceite en una olla y freír la cebolla hasta que esté transparente.

A continuación, añadir el romero, el tomate y la carne. Sazonar con sal y pimienta, revolver con una cuchara de madera y cocinar a fuego bajo durante 15 minutos. Incorporar el arroz, mezclar y rociar con el vino y el caldo, teniendo en cuenta que la mezcla de estos dos líquidos debe duplicar la cantidad del volumen de arroz. Revolver ligeramente y cocinar a fuego bajo durante 20 minutos.

Arroz Marinero

Ingredientes para 6 personas:
500 g de arroz
7 cucharadas de aceite
2 dientes de ajo picados
1 cebolla mediana picada
4 calamares pequeños cortados en aros
500 g de cangrejos de mar
150 g de camarones pelados y desvenados
150 g de arvejas congeladas
Caldo de cocer las cáscaras de los camarones (el doble del volumen de arroz)
Jugo de 1/2 limón
2 pimientos rojos enlatados cortados en trocitos
1/2 cucharadita de color ~ Sal

Calentar el aceite en una paellera y rehogar los ajos y la cebolla hasta que ésta esté transparente. Agregar los calamares y los cangrejos, salar y rehogar durante 8 ó 10 minutos.

A continuación, incorporar los camarones, las arvejas y el arroz, revolver y rociar con el caldo. Añadir el jugo de limón, los pimientos y el colorante, rectificar la sazón y cocinar hasta que el arroz esté en su punto.

Arroz con Conejo

Ingredientes para 4 personas:

400 g de arroz de grano redondo
2 cubitos de caldo de res
2 litros de agua
6 cucharadas de aceite
1 conejo de 2 lb, despresado
2 dientes de ajo pelados
1 cebolla mediana picada
1 pimiento rojo, asado y cortado en tiras
3 cucharadas de pasta de tomate
1 ramita de tomillo
1 hoja de laurel

Hacer un caldo con los cubitos y el agua.

Calentar el aceite en una olla y dorar el conejo. Añadir los ajos y la cebolla y rehogar hasta que ésta esté transparente. Incorporar el pimiento, la pasta de tomate, el tomillo y el laurel. Rociar con el caldo, tapar y cocinar a fuego bajo durante 40 minutos.

Por último, rectificar la sazón, agregar el arroz y cocinar durante 20 minutos. Si fuera necesario, añadir más líquido ya que debe quedar caldoso. Servir de inmediato.

Caldereta de Arroz

Ingredientes para 4 personas:
400 g de arroz ~ 4 cigalas
12 langostinos ~ 1 1/2 litros de agua
2 cubitos de caldo de pescado ~ 4 cucharadas de aceite
1 cebolla picada ~ 2 tomates pelados y picados
1 pimiento rojo enlatado, cortado en tiras ~ 1/2 lb de almejas
1 cucharada de color
100 g de arvejas cocidas ~ Sal

Pelar las cigalas y los langostinos, desvenarlos, reservar las colas y cocinar las cabezas y las cáscaras con el agua y los cubitos de caldo, durante 5 minutos. Colar y reservar el caldo.

A continuación, calentar el aceite y freír la cebolla con los tomates y el pimiento. Cuando todo esté bien frito, añadir las almejas y una vez que éstas se abran, incorporar el caldo reservado, el color y el arroz. Cocinar durante 15 minutos.

Por último, rectificar la sazón, añadir las cigalas, los langostinos y las arvejas y cocinar durante 2 minutos. Retirar del fuego, dejar reposar durante 5 minutos y servir. Debe quedar caldoso.

Arroz Frito con Pollo

Ingredientes para 4 personas:
250 g de arroz de grano largo
3 cucharadas de aceite
1 cebolla pequeña
2 tomates maduros, pelados y picados
350 g de carne de pollo cocida, cortada en trozos
1 cucharada de salsa de soya
2 cucharadas de vino blanco
Sal

Cocinar el arroz en abundante agua con sal hasta que esté en su punto. Colar y reservar.

A continuación, calentar el aceite en una sartén y rehogar la cebolla hasta que esté transparente. Añadir los tomates y rehogar durante 5 minutos.

Por último, incorporar el arroz y los ingredientes restantes, sazonar y cocinar a fuego bajo durante 10 ó 15 minutos, revolviendo frecuentemente con una cuchara de madera.

Servir de inmediato.

Molde de Arroz con Marisco

Ingredientes para 4 personas:

*200 g de arroz de grano largo ~ 300 g de camarones cocidos
1/2 lb de chipi-chipi ~ 3 cucharadas de aceite
2 cebollas largas picadas
1 diente de ajo picado ~ 2 cucharadas de perejil picado
Sal y pimienta ~ Salsa rosa, para acompañar*

Cocinar el arroz en abundante agua con sal hasta que esté en su punto. Colar y reservar.

Mientras tanto, pelar, desvenar los camarones y reservar. Poner los chipi-chipi en un recipiente al fuego hasta que se abran. Separar de las conchas y reservar.

A continuación, calentar el aceite en una sartén y rehogar la cebolla y el ajo hasta que comiencen a dorarse. Añadir los camarones picados (reservar algunos enteros para acompañamiento) y cocinar durante 1 minuto.

Incorporar el arroz, el perejil y los chipi-chipi. Sazonar con sal y pimienta y rehogar todo junto durante 3 ó 4 minutos.

Por último, rellenar 4 moldes pequeños con la preparación. Desmoldar sobre los platos y servir acompañados de los camarones reservados y la salsa rosa, decorando el plato a su elección.

Rissotto Mixto

Ingredientes para 4 personas:
*250 g de arroz de grano largo
2 cucharadas de aceite
1 cebolla picada
1 lb de carne molida de cerdo
1 pimiento verde picado
100 g de orejones remojados y cortados en trozos
Cáscara rallada de 1 naranja
1 cubito de caldo de gallina
3 tazas de agua ~ 1 cucharadita de orégano
Sal y pimienta
Rodajas de naranja, para decorar*

Calentar el aceite en una olla y rehogar la cebolla hasta que esté transparente.

A continuación, añadir la carne, sazonar con sal y pimienta y cocinar, sin dejar de revolver, hasta que esté suelta. Incorporar el pimiento y rehogar durante 10 ó 15 minutos más.

Por último, incorporar el arroz y los ingredientes restantes, revolver y cocinar a fuego bajo durante 20 minutos. Servir de inmediato, decorado con las rodajas de naranja.

Arroz Negro

Ingredientes para 4 personas:
250 g de arroz de grano redondo
5 cucharadas de aceite
1 cebolla pequeña finamente picada
2 tomates maduros pelados y finamente picados
1/2 lb de calamares pequeños muy picados (reservar las bolsitas de tinta)
1 pimiento rojo pequeño seco, remojado
2 dientes de ajo
Agua o caldo de pescado (el doble del volumen de arroz)
50 g de camarones pelados, cocidos y desvenados
Sal

Calentar el aceite en una paellera y sofreír la cebolla y los tomates, revolviendo frecuentemente.

A continuación, agregar los calamares y el pimiento previamente triturado con los ajos. Añadir la tinta de los calamares disuelta en un poquito de agua y el arroz. Mezclar todo bien y rociar con el agua o el caldo. Sazonar con sal y pimienta y cocinar a fuego bajo durante 15 ó 20 minutos.

Por último, retirar del fuego, dejar reposar durante 5 minutos, bien cubierto y servir decorado con los camarones.

Indice de recetas

Arroz a la Campesina, 8-9
Arroz a la Cubana, 12-13
Arroz al Vino Tinto, 14-15
Arroz con Conejo, 18-19
Arroz con Embutidos, 4-5
Arroz Delicioso, 10-11
Arroz Frito con Pollo, 22-23
Arroz Marinero, 16-17
Arroz Negro, 28-29
Caldereta de Arroz, 20-21
Molde de Arroz con Marisco, 24-25
Paella, 6-7
Rissotto Mixto, 26-27